THE LAST YEARS OF
LONDON
STEAM

PETER TUFFREY

GREAT NORTHERN

ACKNOWLEDGEMENTS

Thanks are due to the following people: Roger Arnold; Rosemary Brooksbank; David Burrill; R.W. Carroll; John Chalcraft; Paul Chancellor; David Christie; D.J. Dippie; Peter Gale; David Joy; John Law; Hugh Parkin; Tony at Rail-Online; Bill Reed; Gerald T. Robinson; Sue, Andrew and Rachel Warnes; Tony Watson; Bill Wright.

Great Northern Books
PO Box 1380, Bradford, BD5 5FB
www.greatnorthernbooks.co.uk

Every effort has been made to acknowledge correctly and contact the copyright holders of material in this book. Great Northern Books Ltd apologises for any unintentional errors or omissions, which should be notified to the publisher.

ISBN: 978-1-914227-23-3

Design and layout: David Burrill

CIP Data
A catalogue for this book is available from the British Library

INTRODUCTION

Perhaps the most diverse railway scene in the British Isles was to be found in the London area. This is likely not surprising, given the city's importance as the capital of England and the seat of decision-making for Britain, as well as a large Empire in the late 19th and early 20th centuries. From the earliest days of the railways, connection to London had been a principal consideration, as well as joining different parts of the area for the communication of both passengers and freight.

The first railway in the capital was the London & Greenwich Railway and the line connected the City and Greenwich. An ambitious part of the proposal, which failed to occur, was to run further on to Gravesend or Dover. Small sections were gradually opened owing to the engineering necessary, mainly viaducts carrying the line over streets, rivers and canals. The first was ready for traffic between Spa Road, Bermondsey, and Deptford on 8th February 1836. London Bridge became the western terminus at the end of the year and this is the oldest of the major stations in the capital. Another early local line was the London & Croydon Railway which connected with the L&GR in 1839. Interestingly, Croydon boasted an early plateway which transported minerals and goods to the River Thames at Wandsworth.

In the late 1830s and early 1840s, several long-distance schemes came to fruition. The first was the London & Birmingham Railway, which opened fully from mid-September 1838, though sections had been operational for more than a year. In Birmingham, the line joined with the Grand Junction Railway and this linked with the Liverpool & Manchester Railway to provide continuous services between the capital and Lancashire, as well as major places between. On 11th May 1840, the London & Southampton Railway carried travellers between the two places, initially with a London terminus at Nine Elms. The first part of the Great Western Railway from Paddington to Maidenhead was opened in June 1838, steadily progressing through to Bristol in June 1841. A short time later the London & Brighton Railway reached the South Coast, using London & Croydon as a stepping stone to the destination. Like the Great Western, the Eastern Counties Railway was a steady, long-term project into East Anglia and reached Colchester in 1843 and made a junction with the Norfolk Railway to allow access to Norwich. The South Eastern Railway was obliged to save costs and stop disruption from construction by sharing the London & Brighton line to Tonbridge, then heading eastward to Dover. Traffic ran on the whole length of line from early 1844.

Although the Northern & Eastern Railway proposed to connect London with York on the eastern side of England (a circuitous route via the Midlands and the L&BR line was available), this project stalled and the Great Northern Railway was formed to exploit this area. After completing much of the northern section in the late 1840s, the line from London – originally at Maiden Lane until 1852 when King's Cross opened – was ready in 1850 and a connection was made with the York & North Midland to reach the aforementioned city. The Midland Railway built a formidable territory in the Midlands and Northern England and used the London & Birmingham Railway for access to London. When this became unfavourable, the company diverted on to the GNR line and terminated at King's Cross for a time before the construction of St Pancras in the early 1860s. The last major trunk route into the capital was the 'London Extension' of the Manchester, Sheffield & Lincolnshire Railway in the 1890s, with Marylebone the terminus and the company becoming the Great Central Railway.

As the major lines became established, thoughts turned to connecting these to allow free transfer of freight and passengers. The North London Railway was a scheme of the late 1840s promoted to connect the London & North Western Railway (the successor of the London & Birmingham) with the docks at Poplar in East London. This was completed relatively quickly in 1850. By the end of the decade, the line had been extended to join the North & South Western Junction Railway. The latter was opened in 1853 between the LNWR at Willesden and Brentford on the London & South Western (successor of the London & Southampton).

An early scheme which proved unsuccessful was the West London Railway. Running from the LNWR east of Willesden, the route reached to the Kensington Canal via the GWR main line and was operational for all of six months before closure. The line later became part of an extension to Chelsea and was carried over the Thames to Clapham Junction where the L&SWR and London, Brighton & South Coast Railway was met. This was ready for service in 1863. The need to connect lines and the requirement to do so without taking valuable surface space, led to the creation of the first underground railway, the Metropolitan. This ran from Paddington to King's Cross, then to Farringdon Street just outside the City. The success of the project resulted in expansion of the original lines ('City and Widened Lines') and growth in the route served by such a railway.

As time progressed, the major railway companies dominated the area and consolidated their position. Several improved their running lines owing to increased traffic and this often cascaded into station alterations and rebuilding. Such projects were carried out at Liverpool Street, Waterloo, Victoria, etc.

The Last Years of London Steam visits many of the aforementioned lines, stations, sheds and points between to celebrate the diverse steam scene around London before dieselisation in the late 1960s. Using a number of high-quality colour and black-and-white images, the book features pre-Grouping locomotives still in existence, as well as those of the 'Big Four' – London, Midland & Scottish, London & North Eastern, Southern and Great Western Railways – not excluding the Standard Classes of British Railways. Many of the premier express locomotives are pictured at their respective terminus such as 'Princess Royal' and 'Coronation' Pacifics at Euston, Gresley A3 and A4 Pacifics at King's Cross, Bulleid 'Merchant Navy' and 'Battle of Britain/West Country' Pacifics at Waterloo, and 'King' and 'Castle' Class 4-6-0s at Paddington. Assisting on secondary expresses were LMSR 'Jubilee' Class 4-6-0s, Peppercorn A1 Pacifics and 'Lord Nelson'/'King Arthur' 4-6-0s. Also departing from the many termini were suburban trains, with several dozen Gresley N2s at King's Cross for the task, whilst the ex-GER lines mainly had Hill N7 0-6-2Ts in use. Fowler, Stanier and Fairburn 4P 2-6-4Ts were often running out of Euston with these trains, as well as empty stock movements, which formed a significant amount of traffic to and from the terminus.

Away from the stations, the locomotives are pictured at a number of the large depots used for both stabling and servicing: Bricklayers Arms; Camden; Cricklewood; Feltham; Hither Green; Nine Elms; etc. Many of these were next to the capital's large freight depots and marshalling yards, allowing a number of freight classes not seen in stations to be captured. Also, a number of stations, not to forget freight yards, featured have been lost since the days of steam. Several locomotives survived past the introduction of diesels under London Transport and these are seen just outside the main period presented. As the end drew ever closer, engines were often engaged on enthusiasts' specials, with many leaving the capital for destinations across England, in addition to those on branches and lines crossing London.

Several hundred photographs have been sifted through to assemble this collection, taking many hours, not just because of the editorial process, but the fascinating scenes contained within them. Hopefully, the reader enjoys as many hours perusing through *The Last Years of London Steam* as the author.

Peter Tuffrey
Doncaster, March 2022

Above ACTON – NO. 30520

Urie H16 Class 4-6-2T no. 30520 has a transfer freight train at Acton (on the ex-North & South Western Junction line) in August 1959. Photograph courtesy R.W. Carroll.

Below BARKINGSIDE STATION

Opened by the Great Eastern Railway in 1903, Barkingside station was transferred to the Central line just before Nationalisation. This image dates from 1st April 1961. Photograph by B.W.L. Brooksbank.

Above BARKING STATION – NO. 41948
Thomas Whitelegg produced the 73 Class 4-4-2T locomotive for services on the London, Tilbury & Southend Railway line in the early 20th century. Though just four were built initially, further orders were placed at and after Grouping in 1923. No. 41948 was amongst a group built by Derby Works in 1927 and entered traffic in June of that year. The engine is pictured at Barking station in the late 1940s/early 1950s and has the 'British Railways' lettering on the tender side in the small style. A long-term employee at Plaistow shed, no. 41948 worked there under BR to withdrawal in February 1959. Photograph courtesy Rail-Online.

Opposite above BALHAM STATION – NO. 42091
Balham station opened on 1st December 1856 as Balham Hill. This was part of the West End of London & Crystal Palace Railway which ran from Wandsworth, where a junction was hoped for with the London & South Western Railway, and Crystal Palace to meet the London, Brighton & South Coast Railway. The latter took operational duties and formally absorbed the route subsequently, whilst the L&SWR rejected running rights and an independent extension was made to Battersea Wharf. Fairburn 4P Class 2-6-4T no. 42091 passes through Balham station with a local train for Oxted during August 1959. The engine was new to the Southern Region in April 1951 and at the time of the image was soon to transfer to the London Midland Region at Neasden. Photograph by A. Morris courtesy of Colour-Rail.

Opposite below BARBICAN STATION – NO. L94
Though the use of steam traction officially ended in August 1968, a number of locomotives lingered on past this date. London Transport kept several ex-Great Western Railway 0-6-0PT in use for engineering trains and other freight duties until mid-1971. The last train is pictured here at Barbican station on 6th June when a ballast train ran from Moorgate to Neasden depot, where an open day was taking place. The engine is L94 which was purchased from British Railways in 1959 and after withdrawal was preserved. Photograph by Gordon Edgar courtesy Rail Photoprints.

Opposite above BERRYLANDS STATION – NO. 30925

Richard Maunsell produced a powerful 4-4-0 for the secondary expresses of the Southern Railway. In the early 1930s, the company produced a total of 40 locomotives, designated Class V. The engines were subsequently referred to as the 'Schools' Class following the naming policy adopted of taking those from public schools. No. 30925 *Cheltenham* was built at Eastleigh Works in April 1934. The locomotive is at Berrylands station on 25th August 1962 with a boat train destined for London – note the two Pullman carriages in the formation. No. 30925 was condemned in December 1962 and preserved as part of the National Collection of locomotives. Photograph courtesy Rail-Online.

Opposite below BARKING STATION – NO. 2511

Barking station was opened by the London, Tilbury & Southend Railway in April 1854. This point was important for the line as the tracks diverged east of the station to reach Tilbury Docks and Southend-on-Sea. As a result, the route increased in importance as the railways developed and Barking was rebuilt in 1889, as well as during the 1950s. In the latter period, BR built a flyover and dive-under to allow the free-flow of traffic, as well as completely upgrading the signalling. Stanier 3-cylinder 2-6-4T no. 2511 approaches the station on 25th September 1948 with a Fenchurch Street to Shoeburyness train. Photograph by B.W.L. Brooksbank.

Below BARNES STATION

The Richmond Railway made a junction with the London & South Western Railway at Battersea and ran to Richmond in the early 1840s. The public opening occurred on 27th July 1846 after the work was completed under the direction of Joseph Locke. The station is seen on 7th April 1962 looking westward to Rocks Lane Bridge. Nestled behind this on the right is the 'Tudor gothic' station house which is Grade II listed and the only survivor of the line's five original stations. Photograph by B.W.L. Brooksbank.

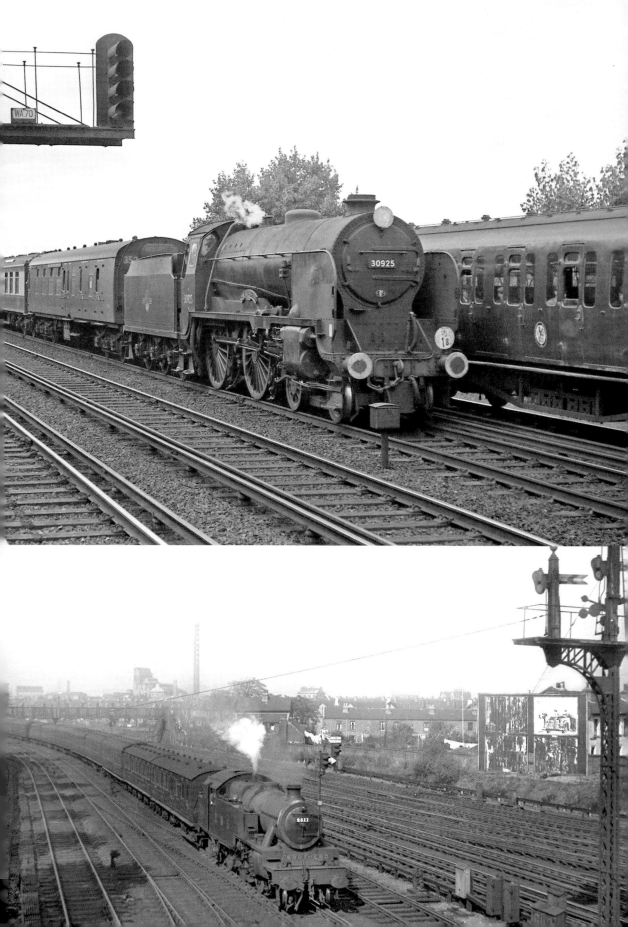

Above BERRYLANDS – NO. 34060

O.V.S. Bulleid became the Chief Mechanical Engineer of the Southern Railway in 1938, leaving the London & North Eastern Railway and his position as assistant to Sir Nigel Gresley. Several of the innovative projects and experiments on the LNER had been performed under Bulleid and he continued this with even more vigour in his new role. His first SR design was the 'Merchant Navy' Pacific which incorporated several 'exotic' features, such as chain-driven valve gear, thermic syphons in the firebox, high boiler pressure and 'air-smoothed' boiler casing. Twenty 'Merchant Navy' Pacifics were erected in the early 1940s, followed by a lighter general service design with similar features. These became known as the 'West Country', 'Battle of Britain' or 'Light' Pacifics and 110 were erected. Bulleid 'Battle of Britain' Class Pacific no. 34060 *25 Squadron* passes through Berrylands during July 1966. The locomotive was employed at Eastleigh and withdrawn during June 1967. Photograph courtesy Rail Photoprints.

Opposite BETHNAL GREEN STATION – NO. 69602

A suburban service from Liverpool Street station reaches Bethnal Green during August 1957 behind Hill N7 Class 0-6-2T no. 69602. Photograph from the Dave Cobbe Collection courtesy Rail Photoprints.

BETHNAL GREEN STATION – NO. 69636
In July 1960, N7 Class no. 69636 is at Bethnal Green station. Photograph by Bill Reed.

Above BETHNAL GREEN STATION – NO. 69723
Hill N7 Class no. 69723 pauses at Bethnal Green station with an Enfield Town to Liverpool Street station, c. 1960. Photograph by Bill Reed.

Below BETHNAL GREEN STATION – NO. 69636
A Chingford to Liverpool Street service is at Bethnal Green station, c. 1960. Running tender first is Hill N7 Class no. 69636. Photograph by Bill Reed.

Above BRICKLAYERS ARMS SHED – NO. 30930

'Schools' Class 4-4-0 no. 30930 *Radley* is over the pits at Bricklayers Arms shed during 1962. Redhill depot's '75B' code is on the smokebox door and this covered the period February to December of 1962. The engine was briefly at Brighton before condemned at the end of the year. Photograph by Bill Reed.

Opposite above BICKLEY STATION – NO. 61329

The 08.35 Victoria to Ramsgate speeds through Bickley station behind Thompson B1 no. 61329 on 22nd May 1953. This Eastern Region engine had been drafted to assist with the motive power shortage which occurred after the Bulleid Pacifics developed a fault. Photograph by N. Sprinks courtesy of Colour-Rail.

Opposite below BRICKLAYERS ARMS SHED – NO. 34014

Though Bulleid's Pacific design was innovative, experience of the locomotive in service found several problems reduced their reliability. British Railways took the decision to reconstruct the class with conventional features and components in the mid-1950s. All the 'Merchant Navy' Class was dealt with, whilst 60 of the 'Light' Pacifics were rebuilt. 'West Country' Pacific no. 34014 *Budleigh Salterton* was amongst this number and transformed in early 1958. The locomotive is at Bricklayers Arms shed on 23rd August 1960. Photograph by D.J. Dippie.

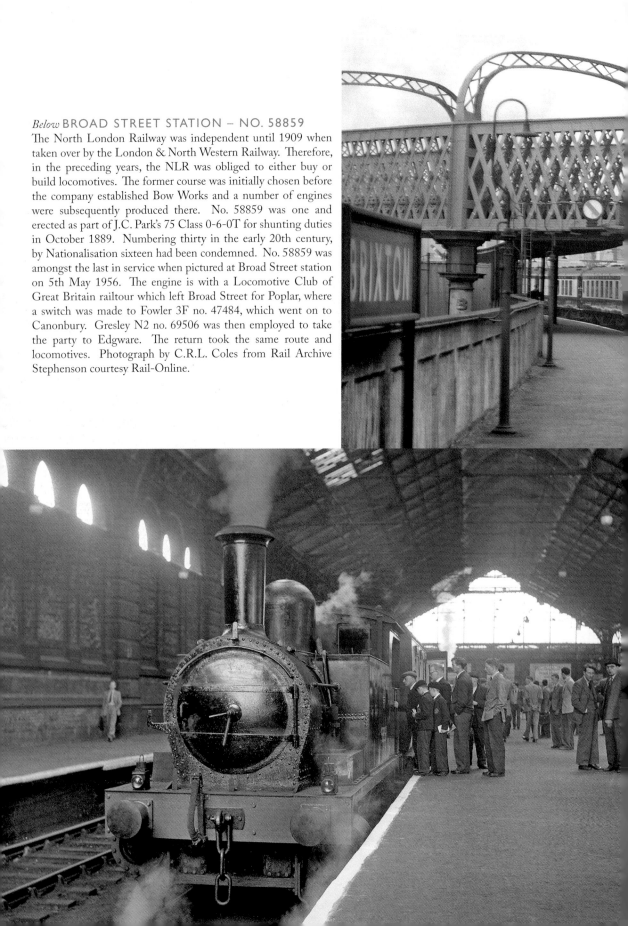

Below BROAD STREET STATION – NO. 58859

The North London Railway was independent until 1909 when taken over by the London & North Western Railway. Therefore, in the preceding years, the NLR was obliged to either buy or build locomotives. The former course was initially chosen before the company established Bow Works and a number of engines were subsequently produced there. No. 58859 was one and erected as part of J.C. Park's 75 Class 0-6-0T for shunting duties in October 1889. Numbering thirty in the early 20th century, by Nationalisation sixteen had been condemned. No. 58859 was amongst the last in service when pictured at Broad Street station on 5th May 1956. The engine is with a Locomotive Club of Great Britain railtour which left Broad Street for Poplar, where a switch was made to Fowler 3F no. 47484, which went on to Canonbury. Gresley N2 no. 69506 was then employed to take the party to Edgware. The return took the same route and locomotives. Photograph by C.R.L. Coles from Rail Archive Stephenson courtesy Rail-Online.

Above BRIXTON STATION – NO. 70004

BR Standard Class 7 'Britannia' Pacific no. 70004 *William Shakespeare* travels southward through Brixton station with the 'Golden Arrow' service from Victoria to Folkestone on 5th October 1957. Until just five years earlier, the traditional destination for the train was Dover to make the crossing to Calais, whilst the return was made to Folkestone. The train is passing under the South London Line between Victoria and London Bridge stations. Photograph by John Head from Rail Archive Stephenson courtesy Rail-Online.

Riley

Above BROMLEY SOUTH STATION – NO. 30795

A development of Robert Urie's H15 Class H15 4-6-0, the N15 was introduced for the London & South Western Railway's heavy passenger traffic towards the end of the First World War. Up to 1926 a total of 74 was constructed. After Grouping, a naming policy was adopted for express engines and the N15s received those from Arthurian legend, resulting in the unofficial title for the class, 'King Arthur'. No. 30795 *Sir Dinadan* was the product of Eastleigh Works in April 1926. The engine is leaving Bromley South station on 25th May 1958 when working from Stewarts Lane shed. Before condemned during August 1962, no. 30795 had spells at Feltham and Basingstoke. Photograph by R.C. Riley courtesy Rail-Online.

Opposite BROMLEY SOUTH STATION – NO. 34091

The Southern Railway ordered 20 Bulleid 'Light' Pacifics before the company was absorbed into British Railways. This brought the class total to 90, yet BR saw fit to request the construction of another 20 locomotives in early 1949. Material shortages and shop capacities delayed the construction of these and the first did not appear until September. This was 'West Country' Class no. 34091 *Weymouth* which was new to Stewarts Lane depot. The engine is pictured here passing through Bromley South station during the 1950s. On the main line between Victoria and Dover, the station was opened by the London, Chatham & Dover Railway on 5th July 1858 as Bromley, though at the turn of the century became Bromley South. No. 34091 had just 15 years in service before condemned at Salisbury in September 1964. Photograph courtesy Colour-Rail.

Above BROMLEY STATION – NO. 47514

A short trip freight is at Bromley station in 1958. The facility was on the London, Tilbury & Southend Railway from 1858 and later had a connection with the North London Railway. Fowler 3F Class 0-6-0 no. 47514 has come off the latter with the train. The engine was based at the nearby Devons Road depot, though in mid-1958 moved on to Camden. In the late 1960s, the station's name was changed to Bromley-by-Bow. Photograph courtesy Rail Photoprints.

Opposite CAMDEN – NO. 42350

A train of empty coaching stock passes through Camden on the way to Euston station on 5th June 1962. The locomotive is Fowler 4P Class 2-6-4T no. 42350, which left Willesden for Birkenhead in 1963 and soon after went to Chester. In 1964 a move to Stafford occurred and no. 42350 was condemned in February 1965. Photograph from the Dave Cobbe Collection, courtesy Rail Photoprints.

Above CAMDEN – NO. 46509

For around a mile out of Euston station the gradients were adverse for northbound trains, ranging between 1 in 70, 1 in 112 and 1 in 77. Ivatt 2MT Class 2-6-0 no. 46509 has dragged a train up in the incline in October 1965. By the end of the month, the engine had been transferred away from Willesden shed after nearly eight months' employment. A year was subsequently spent at Tyseley and Bescot, then being condemned in October 1966. Photograph courtesy R.W. Carroll.

Opposite CAMDEN – NO. 78039

BR Standard Class 2 2-6-0 no. 78039 is at Camden with a train of empty stock bound for Wembley in September 1965. A total of 65 class members were built, all by Darlington Works between 1952 and 1956. The Standard Class 2 was a development of a design from H.G. Ivatt for the London Midland & Scottish Railway, mainly for local trains, both passenger and freight. No. 78039 was new to Rhyl in November 1954 for use on trains between Bangor, Chester and Denbigh. The locomotive was later amongst the group transferred from Rhyl to Widnes. After several years there, no. 78039 moved to Willesden and was amongst 11 which had congregated there by 1965. The class was used on light duties, shunting, local freight and empty stock moves. When the depot closed in September 1965, no. 78039 found work at Shrewsbury. Withdrawal occurred in October 1966. Photograph by J. Dewing from the Dave Cobbe Collection courtesy Rail Photoprints.

© C.R.L. Coles/Rail Archive Stephenson

Above CAMDEN SHED – NO. 45688

Either side of the main line in Camden, facilities serving the railway were present. Two carriage sheds were sited on the east and west sides, whilst a locomotive shed was also located on the curve towards Willesden. The first Camden shed was built on the north side of the curve by the London & Birmingham Railway in 1837 but was replaced on the same location by a roundhouse a decade later. In 1871 this was too small to accommodate locomotives of the time (becoming a gin warehouse, later a live music venue) and a five-road straight shed was erected on the south side of the curve. The LMSR upgraded this to seven tracks in the early 1930s. Stanier 'Jubilee' Class 4-6-0 no. 45688 *Polyphemus* has the smokebox cleaned at Camden c. 1960. In early 1966, the depot closed to steam but the site has continued in railway use. Photograph by C.R.L. Coles from Rail Archive Stephenson courtesy Rail-Online.

Opposite CAMDEN – NO. 75030

A 4-6-0 in the '4' power classification was almost overlooked by BR. The LMSR was well-served by 2-6-0s and 2-6-4Ts, yet other areas of BR, particularly the Western Region and the Cambrian line in Wales, required such a locomotive. Swindon constructed a total of 80 between 1951 and 1956. No. 75030 was in traffic from June 1953 and for a year was at Bletchley. The locomotive then went to Llandudno Junction, though reached Willesden in early 1960 and had three years there. No. 75030 has been caught here on 4th August 1962 with empty coaching stock on Camden incline. The engine was based at Stoke from late 1963 and was condemned there in December 1967. Photograph from the Dave Cobbe Collection courtesy Rail Photoprints.

Above CHELSEA & FULHAM – NO. 41312

A short distance to the south of Chelsea & Fulham station, Ivatt Class 2MT no. 41312 has a Kensington Olympia to Clapham Junction service in June 1967. The signal box present controlled entry to Chelsea basin goods yards. Photograph from the Dave Cobbe Collection courtesy Rail Photoprints.

Opposite CHARING CROSS STATION – NO. 30913

Maunsell 'Schools' Class 4-4-0 no. 30913 *Christ's Hospital* is at Charing Cross station's platform one with a passenger train on 12th April 1958. Working from Ramsgate at this time, the locomotive moved on to Nine Elms in June 1959 and was withdrawn from there in January 1962. Charing Cross station dates from 11th January 1864 when the South Eastern Railway extended the line from London Bridge, also making a connection with the London & South Western's Waterloo station. Designed by Sir John Hawkshaw, Charing Cross was built on a brick viaduct and the six platforms were covered by a single-span roof. Part of this later collapsed in 1905 during refurbishment works, killing six. The entire roof was subsequently replaced and the station has undergone several refurbishments to the present. Photograph courtesy Rail-Online.

Above CLAPHAM JUNCTION STATION – NO. 80095

Dating from May 1838, Clapham Junction station was opened as Wandsworth by the London & South Western Railway. In 1846, the name was changed to Clapham Common, then with the opening of the West London Extension Railway, the station was rebuilt and rechristened Clapham Junction on 2nd March 1863. An interchange with the London, Brighton & South Coast Railway also began at this time. The connection with the WLER allowed the transfer of trains with the London & North Western Railway and a goods station was established by the company at Clapham. BR Standard Class 4 2-6-4T no. 80095 is at Clapham Junction on 20th October 1965. Built at Brighton Works in November 1954 and new to St Albans, by 1965 the engine had undergone several transfers and settled at Nine Elms for the final two years in traffic. The end came in October 1966. Photograph courtesy Colour-Rail.

Below CLAPHAM – NO. 34032
A boat train for Southampton Dock is westbound through Clapham in September 1965. At the head of the service is Bulleid 'West Country' Pacific no. 34032 *Camelford*. Constructed with an 'air-smoothed' casing and standard features at Brighton Works in June 1946, the locomotive has been a participant of BR's rebuilding scheme with conventional features. This took place in October 1960 and saw the engine through to withdrawal in October 1966. For three years prior to this date, no. 34032 was engaged at Salisbury depot. Photograph from the Dave Cobbe Collection courtesy Rail Photoprints.

Above CRICKLEWOOD SHED – NO. 70049

In the company of two new diesel locomotives, 'Britannia' Pacific no. 70049 *Solway Firth* is at Cricklewood shed for servicing on 26th August 1962. In just over two years, the depot was to close to steam following 80 years of stabling engines at the site, which was just to the north of Cricklewood station. A roundhouse was built on the north side of the curve off the branch to Willesden in 1882 for the Midland Railway. Eleven years later, this was joined by a second roundhouse. Following the closure of the site as a diesel service centre, carriage maintenance facilities were established in the old goods yard adjacent to the shed. Photograph courtesy Rail-Online.

Opposite above CLAPHAM JUNCTION STATION – NO. 82019

An engineman climbs on the front of BR Standard Class 3 2-6-2T no. 82019 to change the headcode at Clapham Junction station in early July 1967. Photograph courtesy Colour-Rail.

Opposite below CLAPHAM JUNCTION STATION – NO. 30249

Clapham Junction served as a storage point for empty coaching stock and locomotives were engaged in moving carriages between there and Waterloo. One of these frequent workings is seen at Clapham Junction in October 1958. The locomotive is Drummond M7 no. 30249. Photograph from the Dave Cobbe Collection courtesy Rail Photoprints.

Above EAST CROYDON STATION – NO. 80038

In March 1962, BR Standard Class 4 2-6-4T no. 80038 passes through East Croydon station. This was built by the London & Brighton Railway and ready for traffic on 12th July 1841. Opened as Croydon originally, the L&BR merged with the London & Croydon Railway in 1846 leaving two Croydon stations operated by the company. The L&BR station became Croydon East and then East Croydon in 1862. Before the turn of the century, East Croydon was comprehensively rebuilt and was for a second time in the early 1990s. Photograph courtesy Colour-Rail.

Opposite CROYDON POWER STATION – NOS 2104 AND 2105

A power station was established at Croydon in 1896 and sited on the west side of the Wimbledon & Croydon Railway opened in 1855. This was operated from 1856 by the London, Brighton & South Coast Railway which formally absorbed the route ten years later. Following the Second World War, a second power station was built, Croydon B, with the original serving as Croydon A to 1972. Peckett & Sons 0-4-0ST locomotives nos 2104 and 2105 are on site at Croydon B Power Station in April 1970. Both were soon to be condemned, yet the pair were subsequently preserved. Croydon B was dispensed with during 1984 and the site cleared for a retail development, though the chimneys continue to stand. The Wimbledon & Croydon Railway has been transformed for use as a tramway. Photograph by John Chalcraft courtesy Rail Photoprints.

ENFIELD TOWN STATION – NO. 69693
A suburban train is ready to leave Enfield Town station for Liverpool Street in July 1960, behind Hill N7 Class 0–6–2T no.69693. Photograph by Bill Reed.

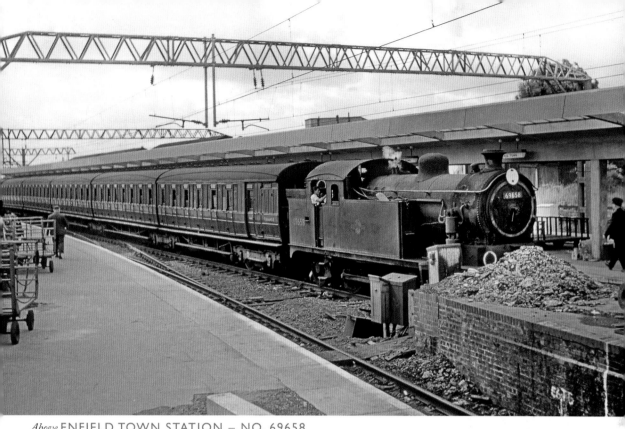

Above ENFIELD TOWN STATION – NO. 69658

At least one quintuplet articulated set is in this train from Liverpool Street which has reached Enfield Town behind N7 no. 69658. Photograph by Bill Reed.

Below ENFIELD TOWN STATION – NO. 69723

Light engine at Enfield Town station is N7 Class no. 69723. Recently, the station had been rebuilt as part of the local electrification scheme. Photograph by Bill Reed.

Above EUSTON STATION – NO. 46207

In 1954, the boat train express between Euston and Liverpool was christened the 'Shamrock'. Leaving Lime Street at 08.10, the service was due around mid-day, whilst the northbound train departed Euston at 16.55. Stanier 'Princess Royal' Pacific no. 46207 *Princess Arthur of Connaught* arrives with the 'Shamrock' on 28th June 1955. The engine was at Edge Hill, Liverpool, for the majority of the 1950s and had two years in London at Willesden and Camden before sent for scrap in November 1961. Photograph by Geoff Warnes.

Opposite above EUSTON STATION – NO. 46115

The 'Mancunian' named train was instigated by the London Midland & Scottish Railway in 1928. The service ran between Euston and Manchester London Road and was initially a mid-morning, late afternoon train. Under BR, the departure was set at 09.45 from Manchester with a timing of 3 hours 35 minutes and 18.00 from Euston, reaching the destination in 3 hours 30 minutes. The morning train could run up to 15-16 coaches and a relief express existed, whilst the northern service generally ran a dozen vehicles. Motive power was typically Fowler 'Royal Scots' and class member no. 46115 *Scots Guardsman* is with the train here during 1958. The engine was Longsight-based at this time. Photograph courtesy Rail-Online.

Opposite below EUSTON STATION – NO. 42068

Circa 1960, Fairburn 4P Class 2-6-4T no. 42068 is at Euston station. A new Class 24 diesel electric is also visible. Although an LMSR design, this 4P was constructed at Brighton Works and found use on the Southern Region, mainly at Ramsgate and Brighton. In December 1959, the engine began a three-and-a-half-year spell at Willesden depot. No. 42068 was condemned after six months at Bushbury in December 1963. Photograph by F. Hornby courtesy of Colour-Rail.

EUSTON STATION – NO. 45604

'Jubilee' no. 45604 *Ceylon* waits for the next duty at Euston on 30th July 1964. The station's reconstruction progress may be seen in the background. Photograph by Chris Davies courtesy Rail Photoprints.

Above and below EUSTON STATION – NO. 45015

On 25th May 1963, two views of Stanier Class Five no. 45015 have been taken, with departure above and preparation occurring for the event below. The locomotive has substituted for failed 'Britannia' no. 70051 *Firth of Forth* on a late evening train from Euston – an FA Cup final special, with Leicester and Manchester United the contestants. No. 45015 was a Liverpool engine at this time and was in service there to September 1967. Photographs by David Christie.

Above EUSTON STATION – NO. 45717
Reversing towards a train at Euston station during April 1963 is 'Jubilee' Class no. 45717 *Dauntless*. Under BR, the locomotive worked from Bank Hall shed, Liverpool, and was condemned there in October. Photograph by David Christie.

Below EUSTON STATION – NO. 42221
A train of empty stock arrives at Euston station behind Fairburn 4P Class 2-6-4T no. 42221 on 12th April 1963. The engine was soon to leave Willesden for Kirkby-in-Ashfield. Photograph by David Christie.

Above EUSTON STATION – NO. 46256

In a break from the set standard of Brunswick green for express passenger locomotives, the London Midland Region allowed the application of LMSR maroon in the late 1950s. Appropriately, 'Coronation' Class Pacific no. 46256 *Sir William A. Stanier F.R.S.* had this applied, with LMSR lining, from May 1958. The engine is arriving at Euston in September 1962. Photograph by David Christie.

Below EUSTON STATION – NO. 48416

As the reconstruction of Euston station progressed in the early 1960s, trains of material and rubble moved to and from the site. Stanier 8F no. 48416 has one such service in June 1963. Photograph by David Christie.

Below EUSTON STATION – NO. 80065

BR Standard Class 4 2-6-4T no. 80065 is at Euston station on 28th June 1955. The engine was just two years old at this time and had left Brighton Works for Watford. Working there for the rest of the decade, no. 80065 welcomed the 1960s at Dover, though soon after transferred to Ashford. For the last four years in traffic, the locomotive was at Eastleigh and withdrawal occurred in September 1966. Photograph by Geoff Warnes.

Above EUSTON STATION – NO. 46170

Euston station was opened for the London & Birmingham Railway in July 1837. Following the formation of the London & North Western Railway in the mid-1840s, additions and improvements were made to Euston in 1849 and further work was carried out through to the 1920s. Plans to rebuild completely were halted by the war, though British Railways carried through the project in the 1960s. The station is still intact here on 18th August 1960 as 'Royal Scot' no. 46170 *British Legion* has arrived with a passenger service. The locomotive began life as no. 6170 *Fury*, which possessed an experimental boiler working at high-pressure. Due to the failure of this project, reconstruction occurred in 1935. At the time of the image, no. 46170 was employed at Crewe and was condemned at Llandudno Junction in December 1962. Photograph by D.J. Dippie.

Brian Stephenson

Above FELTHAM – NO. 73087

A special passenger train passes through Feltham on 3rd November 1956. The locomotive is BR Standard Class 5 no. 73087, which was one of the original class members allocated to the Southern Region at Stewarts Lane. Subsequently, time was spent at work on the Somerset & Dorset Joint line from Bath and no. 73087 was at Eastleigh when pictured. At the end of the 1950s, a number of Southern Region Class 5s were named with those belonging to withdrawn Urie N15 'King Arthur' Class 4-6-0s and no. 73087 was christened *Linette* in June 1961. Photograph courtesy Rail-Online.

Opposite above FARRINGDON STATION – NO. L44

On 1st October 1961 the 'Metropolitan' railtour was organised by the Southern Counties Touring Society. This ran from Wembley to New Cross Gate with London Transport no. L44, which began life as Metropolitan no. 1. Part of the E Class, the engine was one of seven erected between 1896 and 1901. L44 was withdrawn soon after the tour – pictured arriving at Farringdon station – and was later preserved. A permanent home was found for the locomotive at the Buckinghamshire Railway Centre, though L44 has travelled again in London as part of celebrations for anniversaries of several lines. Photograph by Brian Stephenson courtesy Rail-Online.

Opposite below FELTHAM SHED – NO. 31917

The London & South Western Railway established extensive marshalling yards at Feltham just before Grouping. This relieved the burden at Nine Elms and improved transfer of freight to other rail lines. At the yard's height, 5,500 wagons passed through daily and around 150 trains were formed. A depot for locomotives was also built nearby to house and service those arriving and working at the yard. Maunsell W Class 2-6-4T no. 31917 is at the shed on 23rd June 1963 and was a recent arrival there at the start of the year. Photograph by K.C.H. Fairey courtesy of Colour-Rail.

Above FELTHAM SHED – NO. 32408

Billinton E6 Class 0-6-2T no. 32408 is shunting at Feltham shed on 11th March 1961. A recent addition to the ranks there, the locomotive moved from Bricklayers Arms. Brighton Works constructed no. 32408 in December 1904 and the engine was in traffic to the end of 1962 after seven months at Eastleigh. Photograph by Bill Reed.

Opposite FELTHAM SHED

View from the roof of Feltham shed over to the marshalling yard in February 1958. By this time, the importance of Feltham, and that of the railways for the movement of freight traffic, was dwindling and resulted in the closure of the yard in early 1969. In 1958, Feltham shed had around 60 locomotives allocated, mainly S15 Class 4-6-0s, followed by Bulleid Q1 Class 0-6-0s, two of which are seen here, and H16 4-6-2Ts. At this time, BR was introducing a large number of diesel electric shunters, later Class 08, and five are in the yard. Locomotives identifiable are no. 30495, no. 30520 (both H16s) and Q1s, no. 33007 and no. 33011. Feltham shed closed to steam in July 1967 and the site, along with that of the marshalling yard, has since been cleared. Photograph from the Dave Cobbe Collection courtesy Rail Photoprints.

Above FENCHURCH STREET STATION – NO. 80134

A local train arrives at Fenchurch Street station behind BR Standard Class 4 2-6-4T no. 80134 on 21st August 1959. The engine was built at Brighton in April 1956 and new to Plaistow. During November 1959 a transfer to Tilbury occurred and from 1962, no. 80134 was in South Wales at Swansea and Llanelly. Between September 1964 and July 1967, the engine worked at Bournemouth. Photograph by M.J. Reade courtesy of Colour-Rail.

Below

FENCHURCH STREET STATION – NO. 42522

The London & Blackwall Railway opened a station at Fenchurch Street in July 1841, being the first in the City of London. Rebuilding occurred over a decade later and again under the LMSR in the 1930s. Stanier 4P Class 2-6-4T no. 42522 has a parcels train at Fenchurch Street on 22nd August 1960. Photograph courtesy Rail-Online.

Above HADLEY WOOD STATION – NO. 60131
Peppercorn A1 Class Pacific no. 60131 *Osprey* passes Hadley Wood station with a northbound express in 1959. Photograph courtesy R.W. Carroll.

Opposite above FINSBURY PARK – NO. 60533
A northbound express travels through Finsbury Park behind Peppercorn A2 Class Pacific no. 60533 *Happy Knight* during 1962. Photograph from the John Day Collection courtesy Rail Photoprints.

Opposite below GAS FACTORY JUNCTION – NO. 42519
Stanier 4P no. 42519 joins the old road to Fenchurch Street from the 1858 line at Gas Factory Junction, Bow, on 13th June 1959. The 1858 route improved communication between the station and the LT&SR route. Photograph courtesy Rail-Online.

Above **HARRINGAY WEST STATION – NO. 69536**

As the suburbanisation of North London took place, infrastructure changes were necessary. The GNR was obliged to open a station at Harringay for a nearby housing development in the mid-1880s, with funds for this provided by the housing company. In the 1950s, the name changed to Harringay West to differentiate from the station on the Tottenham & Hampstead Junction line which became Harringay Park. Gresley N2/2 Class 0-6-2T no. 69536 has a train of two Gresley quadruple articulated sets passing through Harringay West on their way to Hatfield on 3rd April 1958. Photograph by B.W.L. Brooksbank.

Opposite above **HAMPSTEAD – NO. 73019**

BR Standard Class 5 no. 73019 is northbound through Hampstead with an express on 27th February 1952. Photograph courtesy Rail-Online.

Opposite below **HAMPTON COURT JUNCTION – NO. 33020**

Approaching Hampton Court Junction on the L&SWR main line, Bulleid Q1 no. 33020 has a ballast train on 11th April 1965. Photograph by Ian Turnbull courtesy Rail Photoprints.

Above HARRINGAY WEST STATION – NO. 60500

The 16.21 semi-fast King's Cross to Peterborough train has reached Harringay West behind Thompson A2 Pacific no. 60500 *Edward Thompson* on 11th June 1962. Photograph by Ian Turnbull courtesy Rail Photoprints.

Opposite above HARRINGAY – NO. 68896 AND NO. 68975

Two Gresley J50 Class 0-6-0T locomotives are at Harringay, likely returning from Ferme Park marshalling yard to the nearby shed. No. 68896 is leading, whilst no. 68975 is behind. Photograph by B.W.L. Brooksbank.

Opposite below HARRINGAY – NO. 68077

On 2nd June 1959 a freight train has just left Ferme Park yard behind J94 0-6-0ST no. 68077. Photograph by B.W.L. Brooksbank.

Above HIGH BARNET STATION – NO. 69540

A branch from Finchley to High Barnet opened in 1872 under the Great Northern Railway. During the 1930s, the London Passenger Transport Board planned to expand the Northern Line and this included taking over the High Barnet branch. The first underground trains ran in 1940 and steam passenger services ceased during the following year, though freight continued to the early 1960s. At an unknown date, Gresley N2 Class 0-6-2T no. 69540 has reached High Barnet station with a special passenger service; an underground train is at the opposite platform. Photograph courtesy R.W. Carroll.

Below

HARROW AND WEALDSTONE STATION

At 08.19 on 8th October 1952, the 20.15 overnight express from Perth to Euston collided with a local train on the fast line at Harrow and Wealdstone station. Unfortunately, a northbound express for Liverpool reached the station at the same time and crashed into the wreckage from the first accident. Tragically, 112 were killed and over 300 injured. On 11th October, the engine leading the Perth train, 'Coronation' Class Pacific no. 46242 *City of Glasgow* is recovered after being buried amidst the debris. Both this locomotive and the Fowler 2-6-4T at the head of the local continued in service, whilst the two hauling the Liverpool train were damaged beyond repair. Photograph by W.S. Garth from Rail Archive Stephenson courtesy Rail-Online.

Above HITHER GREEN – NO. 34084

'Battle of Britain' Pacific no. 34084 *253 Squadron* waits to be recovered following a mishap at Hither Green on 21st February 1960. The locomotive was working a freight train at the time and passed through a signal which led to a derailment and falling down this embankment. Eastleigh Works restored the engine and work was resumed at Dover. At the end of the year no. 34084 moved on to Exmouth Junction. Photograph by Bill Reed.

Opposite above HITHER GREEN SHED – NO. 33010

Bulleid's Q1 Class 0-6-0 was the response made to the need for freight locomotives on the Southern Railway during the Second World War. Owing to material shortages, superfluous details were omitted, as on other lines, though the Q1 was perhaps the most 'austere'-looking of all. A total of 40 was constructed in 1942 split equally between Brighton and Ashford Works. No. 33010 was built at the first mentioned and began work in August. The engine is in a particularly presentable condition at Hither Green shed, c. 1960. No. 33010 was Feltham-allocated throughout BR service, which ended in January 1964. Photograph by Bill Reed.

Opposite below HITHER GREEN SHED – NO. 31783

Sited in the triangular junction between the main line to Dover and the Dartford route, Hither Green shed was opened by the Southern Railway in 1933. The building had six roads and a ramped coal stage (seen right), as well as a 65 ft turntable. Maunsell L1 Class 4-4-0 no. 31783 is on site c. 1960. Built by the North British Locomotive Company in April 1926, the engine was in traffic to December 1961. Photograph by Bill Reed.

Above HOLBORN VIADUCT LOW LEVEL – NO. 47203

Approaching the site of the closed Holborn Viaduct Low Level station is Johnson 3F 0-6-0T no. 47203. The station, also known as Snow Hill, was just north of Holborn Viaduct station on the ex-London, Chatham & Dover Railway line between Blackfriars and Farringdon stations. No. 47203 is working a transfer freight on 13th September 1956. Photograph courtesy Rail-Online.

Opposite HITHER GREEN STATION – NO. 31717

The South East & Chatham Railway introduced the C Class 0-6-0 for freight work in the early 20th century. The first appeared in 1900 and construction progressed through to 1908 when 109 examples existed. Several manufacturers were involved, with this locomotive, no. 31717, the product of Sharp, Stewart & Co. in January 1901. The engine was in service just over 60 years and is seen at the end of this time passing through Hither Green station with a mixed freight on 24th April 1961. Photograph from the Dave Cobbe Collection courtesy Rail Photoprints.

Above KENSAL GREEN – NO. 45035

Just west of Kensal Green station, Stanier Class 5 no. 45035 has emerged from Kensal Green tunnel with a train of empty stock on 10th September 1961. A long-term resident of Warrington shed, the engine was briefly at Blackpool and Fleetwood depots before withdrawn in November 1964. Photograph by K.L. Cook from Rail Archive Stephenson courtesy Rail-Online.

Below

HORNSEY STATION – NO. 60869

Gresley V2 Class no. 60869 is the focus of attention at Hornsey station as the locomotive works a Peterborough to King's Cross local train, c. 1960. Constructed at Darlington Works in August 1939, no. 60869 (as LNER no. 4840) was new to King's Cross depot, but moved north to Peterborough in November 1942 and remained until condemned for scrap in June 1963. Photograph courtesy R.W. Carroll.

Above KENSINGTON (OLYMPIA) – NO. 41298

Kensington was the terminus point for the West London Railway in the 1840s. Yet, the line proved a failure and closure occurred soon after. With the scheme to connect Willesden and Clapham Junction, Kensington station was revived and opened again in 1862. When underground stations were built at Kensington, the overground station became Kensington Addison Road. Closure occurred again during the Second World War due to enemy action and when returned to service a further change was made to the name, becoming Kensington (Olympia). A large exhibition venue was promoted in the early 1880s and a site at Kensington was chosen, adjacent to Addison Road station for ease of transport. The building, which is partially visible on the left behind the signal box, was opened in 1886 and has continued to host events to the present. The venue's garage for motor vehicles also highlights the station's decline in importance for travellers reaching Olympia. Ivatt 2MT 2-6-2T no. 41298 has the 08.31 train to Clapham Junction at Kensington on 26th May 1967. Photograph by Ian Turnbull courtesy Rail Photoprints.

Opposite above KING'S CROSS STATION – NO. 60130

On 2nd March 1963 an express has reached King's Cross station behind Peppercorn A1 Pacific no. 60130 *Kestrel*. The locomotive was employed at Leeds Copley Hill depot at this time. Photograph by David Christie.

Opposite below KING'S CROSS STATION

A crowded scene caught at King's Cross station on 3rd September 1962. Gresley A3 Pacific no. 60110 *Robert the Devil* is coupled to Thompson A2/3 Pacific no. 60513 *Dante*, whilst the latter's class mate no. 60522 *Straight Deal* waits to depart with an express. Photograph by David Christie.

Above KING'S CROSS STATION – NO. 60021
Gresley A4 Class Pacific no. 60021 *Wild Swan* reverses out of King's Cross station on 12th April 1963. King's Cross-allocated for the past 13 years, the locomotive was to move in June following the closure of that shed and had four months at Peterborough before sent for scrap. Photograph by David Christie.

Opposite above KING'S CROSS STATION – NO. 60015
Only a month in traffic remained for the second Gresley A4 constructed, no. 60015 *Quicksilver*, which is pictured moving towards a train at King's Cross station on 2nd March 1963. Steam was soon to be banned south of Peterborough, rendering many long-term servants redundant. The locomotive had spent much of the 27 years in traffic working from King's Cross shed on the top expresses and retained a corridor tender throughout to allow service on the non-stop trains. In two seasons, no. 60015 was noted several times at the head of 'The Elizabethan' King's Cross to Edinburgh non-stop. Photograph by David Christie.

Opposite below KING'S CROSS STATION – NO. 60117
The introduction of Gresley's A1 Class Pacifics posed a particular problem for the LNER, as many turntables were too short to turn the locomotives. At King's Cross, the engines had to travel to Hornsey to change their orientation and a 70 ft turntable was not installed at King's Cross until 1924. Further operational problems were caused by the volume of traffic having to pass through Gas Works Tunnel and many locomotives were serviced in the yard in the north-west corner. Depending on the length of times between duties, Peppercorn A1 Pacific no. 60117 *Bois Roussel* was either destined there for the short term or the shed, which was on the other side of the tunnel. The engine was allocated to Copley Hill shed when pictured on 2nd March 1963. Photograph by David Christie.

Above KING'S CROSS STATION – NO. 60022

Equally as recognisable as the famous locomotives that habituated King's Cross station was the signal box which stood at the end of platforms five/six. This was built in the early 1930s to replace two boxes, east and west, the latter of which stood just to the north of the new box. As a preventative measure to avoid the potential of flooding, the new signal box was two storeys. Gresley A4 no. 60022 *Mallard* leaves King's Cross for servicing c. 1960. The locomotive was perhaps the most famous face to be seen at the station owing to the setting of the speed record for steam traction in 1938. A plaque (just visible here) was fitted around Nationalisation attesting to this fact. Photograph courtesy Colour-Rail.

Below KING'S CROSS STATION – NO. 60103
On 16th August 1962, Gresley A3 Pacific no. 60103 *Flying Scotsman* is at the head of a mid-morning express waiting to depart King's Cross. Photograph by D.J. Dippie.

Above KING'S CROSS STATION – NO. 60113
Also at King's Cross station on 16th August 1962 is Thompson A1 Pacific no. 60113 *Great Northern*. Photograph by D.J. Dippie.

Opposite above KING'S CROSS STATION – NO. 69545
One of the many Gresley N2 Class 0-6-2Ts, no. 69545, that worked the suburban services from King's Cross is at the station in 1956 with a train for Finsbury Park. The locomotive was one of fifty class members built by the North British Locomotive Company, emerging from the shops in April 1921. In order to work from King's Cross, the N2s were fitted with condensing apparatus, seen here running from the smokebox to the side tank. Under BR, no. 69545 worked solely from King's Cross depot. Photograph from the John Day Collection courtesy Rail Photoprints.

Opposite below KING'S CROSS STATION – NO. 60105
Grantham-based Gresley A3 Pacific no. 60105 *Victor Wild* is using King's Cross turntable on 23rd August 1960. Peppercorn A1 Pacific no. 60140 *Balmoral* stands behind. Photograph by D.J. Dippie.

Above LIVERPOOL STREET STATION – NO. E8619

For shunting duties at major stations, dedicated locomotives were chosen and often specially decorated. At Liverpool Street, Holden J69 Class 0-6-0T no. E8619 was given this role after Nationalisation. It was turned out from Stratford Works in LNER apple green livery with 'British Railways' on the tender and Eastern Region prefix. In 1953, the engine reverted to the class standard black livery, though later received lining and at the end of the decade was honoured with Great Eastern Railway blue, red coupling rods and burnished metal work. No. E8619 is at work on 22nd April 1952. Photograph by George C. Lander courtesy Rail Photoprints.

Opposite above LIVERPOOL STREET STATION – NO. 61660

Similar to King's Cross station (see below), Liverpool Street had a problem for servicing locomotives. Stratford shed was a distance away and engines with a quick turnaround had to be refreshed at the station. Necessary facilities were provided, including a turntable between Pindar Street and Primrose Street bridges over the running lines. Gresley B17 Class 4-6-0 no. 61660 *Hull City* has use of the turntable in 1955. The engine was Stratford-based at this time. Photograph courtesy Rail Photoprints.

Opposite below KING'S CROSS STATION – NO. 69824

Although King's Cross shed was only on the other side of Gas Works Tunnel (seen here), the volume of traffic occupying the lines meant moves to/from there were limited. King's Cross station had a small area reserved for servicing purposes in the north-west corner and the detritus from the fireboxes of several locomotives has accumulated here on 3rd April 1958. Also present is Robinson A5 Class 4-6-2T no. 69824 which was working at King's Cross on a trial basis to see if the engine improved on the performance of Thompson L1 Class 2-6-4Ts taking heavier trains out to the carriage sidings. This was not the case and no. 69824 went on to find employment at Grantham. Photograph by B.W.L. Brooksbank.

Above LIVERPOOL STREET STATION – NO. 61109

Thompson B1 no. 61109 was completed at the NBLC in December 1946 and new to the LNER's Great Central Section at Darnall, Sheffield. A move to the Great Eastern Section and Stratford occurred in 1949 and lasted 11 years. The locomotive is at Liverpool Street with an express on 10th September 1960, with Hill N7 Class 0-6-2T no. 69654 also visible. Photograph by D.C. Ovenden courtesy of Colour-Rail.

Opposite LIVERPOOL STREET STATION – NO. 70037

This image is looking from the original side of Liverpool Street station to the new in July 1959 and 'Britannia' Pacific no. 70037 *Hereward the Wake* is featured in the servicing area. Photograph from the Dave Cobbe Collection courtesy Rail Photoprints.

Above LIVERPOOL STREET STATION – NO. 61156

On 16th August 1962, Thompson B1 no. 61156 is the odd one out at Liverpool Street station. The engine is surrounded by several diesel locomotives, including Brush Type 2 D5523 (behind), class mate D5597 and English Electric Type 3 D6724 (later Class 37). No. 61156 was built by Vulcan Foundry in May 1947 and was a GC Section engine to 1957 when transferred to the GE Section. Stratford acquired the locomotive in February 1961 and this lasted to September 1962. Withdrawal from March occurred in November 1963. Photograph by D.J. Dippie.

Opposite LIVERPOOL STREET STATION – NO. 70034

This image shows the cab road off Pindar Street and the servicing facilities at Liverpool Street station, with the turntable off to the left. 'Britannia' Class Pacific no. 70034 *Thomas Hardy* features and is between duties during July 1959. Constructed at Crewe Works in December 1952, the locomotive was first allocated to Longsight depot but in July 1953 moved to Stratford and worked the East of England expresses through to 1961. The last two years were spent at Norwich and no. 70034 saw further service on the London Midland Region, being sent for scrap in May 1967. Photograph from the Dave Cobbe Collection courtesy Rail Photoprints.

Above LIVERPOOL STREET STATION – NO. 69730

After the formation of the Great Eastern Railway, Bishopsgate station was declared inadequate and a new facility was needed. Land was found next to Broad Street station off Liverpool Street and work began in 1873 after financial difficulties had been overcome, being completed in 1875 at a cost of over £130,000. The ironwork for Liverpool Street's train shed was provided by Fairburn Engineering Co. and consisted of four spans. Two centrally were 109 ft wide and flanked by two smaller at 45 ft. Expansion was necessary in the 1890s and eight new lines were added on the eastern side of the original station. The 18.10 to Chingford is at the platform at Liverpool Street station on 25th April 1960. A.J. Hill N7 Class 0-6-2T no. 69730 has the train. As mentioned, the design was introduced by the GER in 1915 as the L77 Class and the LNER went on to perpetuate this, though with a round-top firebox. No. 69730 was one of thirty-two erected at Doncaster and entered traffic in November 1928. Photograph by M.J. Reade courtesy of Colour-Rail.

Opposite LONDON BRIDGE STATION – NO. 30925

The Railway Correspondence & Travel Society arranged a tour of Sussex on 10th October 1962. Maunsell 'Schools' Class no. 30925 *Cheltenham* was the lead engine and took the party from London Bridge station to Brighton. The engine is well-presented and ready to depart London Bridge here. Photograph from the Dave Cobbe Collection courtesy Rail Photoprints.

Below LONDON BRIDGE STATION – NO. 30931

Passing through platform seven at London Bridge station on 23rd May 1958 is Maunsell 'Schools' Class no. 30931 *King's – Wimbledon*. After Grouping, the Southern Railway had developed a policy of naming passenger locomotives and this continued with the V Class 4-4-0s taking those of public schools connected with the company's lines. King's College School, Wimbledon, was formed in 1829 by George IV and nearly ten years later Wimbledon station was opened on the first section of the London & South Western Railway's main line. No. 30931 was in service to September 1961 and one of the nameplates was later acquired by the school. Photograph by L. Rowe courtesy of Colour-Rail.

Above LONDON BRIDGE STATION – NO. 75070

One of the oldest London stations, London Bridge was opened by the London & Greenwich Railway in 1836. The London & Croydon was set to use the station, yet space could not be found and the company had to build a new facility adjacent which was ready for traffic in 1839. When the London & Brighton and South Eastern Railways were looking for a station in the capital, they entered into an agreement with the L&CR and a joint station was partially built in the early 1840s. The London, Brighton & South Coast Railway was formed in 1846 and went on to take over the joint station which was rebuilt in the 1850s, whilst the SER took over the L&GR station. The two sides were ultimately united under the Southern Railway and BR rebuilt the whole site in the 1970s. BR Standard Class 4 4-6-0 no. 75070 is at London Bridge on 24th April 1959 with the 16.40 train to East Grinstead via Oxted. Photograph by B.W.L. Brooksbank.

Above LONDON BRIDGE STATION – NO. 42092

A suburban service approaches London Bridge station behind Fairburn 4P 2-6-4T no. 42092 in 1955. The lineage for this class stretched back to 1927 when Sir Henry Fowler introduced a 4P 2-6-4T for medium-distance trains and commuter services. A total of 125 was built to 1934 when Stanier modified the design to feature his own engineering preferences. Initially, he built a three-cylinder version for use on the London, Tilbury & Southend line, yet this proved to be no improvement on the Fowler 4Ps and reverted back and provided two cylinders for future construction, which eventually numbered 206. Fairburn reduced the wheelbase of his 4Ps to improve route availability and this prompted BR to spread the sphere of operation to other areas in need of suitable locomotives. A number of the 277 engines built saw service on the Southern Region, as well as the North Eastern Region. No. 42092 was new to Brighton shed from the local workshops in May 1951 and remained on the SR to 1959 when moved to Neasden. In 1955, the locomotive was Three Bridges-allocated. Photograph from the John Day Collection courtesy Rail Photoprints.

Below LONDON BRIDGE STATION – NO. 30901
On 28th August 1956, Maunsell 'Schools' Class no. 30901 *Winchester* is at London Bridge station heading a passenger service. Photograph by George C. Lander courtesy Rail Photoprints.

Above MARYLEBONE STATION – NO. 75035

Whilst London Bridge was one of the oldest stations in the capital, Marylebone was the last major addition to London's railways in the 19th century. Sir Edward Watkin, who was the Chairman of the Manchester, Sheffield & Lincolnshire Railway, planned from the 1860s to extend the company's line southward to London. Authorisation was not obtained until the early 1890s and the terminus was established west of Regent's Park on an area of over 50 acres. Marylebone station welcomed passengers from March 1899. BR Standard Class 4 4-6-0 no. 75035 is there with an express passenger service in the 1960s. Photograph from the John Day Collection courtesy Rail Photoprints.

Below LOUGHBOROUGH JUNCTION STATION – NO. 31048

The London, Chatham & Dover Railway laid an extension from the main line at Herne Hill to Holborn Viaduct station and this was completed in 1863. In the following year, platforms were established at Loughborough Road, Brixton, for the spur between the extension and the original route to Victoria. In the early 1870s a connection was made to Denmark Hill and Loughborough Junction station was opened at this time. O1 Class 0-6-0 no. 31048 has a freight train passing through the station on 25th May 1959. Photograph courtesy Rail-Online.

Above MARYLEBONE STATION – NO. 45299

Willesden-based Class 5 no. 45299 arrives at Marylebone station with the 08.15 from Nottingham on 26th July 1965. Constructed by Armstrong Whitworth & Co. in January 1937, the engine was in traffic to November 1967. Photograph by Hugh Ballantyne courtesy Rail Photoprints.

Opposite above MARYLEBONE STATION – NO. 60049

The Sheffield-Marylebone train was an important service from the early 20th century and was an early departure tightly timed to reach London in the mid-morning. The return was made early evening and was similarly tough due to the suburban traffic congesting the line. Whilst withdrawn during the war, the train returned in 1947 under the title 'The Master Cutler' to a similar schedule. The northbound service left Marylebone at 18.15 and ran via High Wycombe and Princes Risborough. Expected arrival in Sheffield was around 22.00. Gresley A3 Pacific no. 60049 *Galtee More* has 'The Master Cutler' ready for departure from Marylebone in the early 1950s. The A3s had several spells on the GC Section and were used on the train, in addition to Thompson B1s. No. 60049 mainly worked at Leicester between 1949 and 1957. Photograph by R.A. Whitfield courtesy Rail Photoprints.

Opposite below MARYLEBONE STATION – NO. 44847

Stanier Class 5 no. 44847 has reached Marylebone station with the 08.15 train from Nottingham on 19th September 1964. A major reorganisation of regional boundaries occurred in 1958 which took the GCR's London Extension into the London Midland Region. Annesley shed, Nottingham, was affected by the change and saw an influx of 'foreign' locomotives as older types were ousted or scrapped. At the time, no. 44847 experienced the opposite transfer at Sheffield Millhouses but was soon found a berth at Neasden and continued on the former GCR Section at Leicester and Annesley, where the engine was employed when captured at Marylebone. Photograph by Hugh Ballantyne courtesy Rail Photoprints.

Above MARYLEBONE STATION – NO. 67789
The 18.00 train from Marylebone to Woodford Halse is at the platform on 3rd August 1957 with Thompson L1 Class 2-6-4T no. 67789. The locomotive was amongst 100 built for suburban traffic and was completed by Robert Stephenson & Hawthorn Ltd in May 1950. Originally working at Norwich, no. 67789 moved to Neasden in 1953 and two years later was at Woodford Halse. This remained the case to withdrawal in October 1962. Photograph by M.J. Reade courtesy of Colour-Rail.

Opposite above MARYLEBONE STATION – NO. 44825
Following the transfer of the London Extension to the London Midland Region, plans to run-down services on the route were quickly enacted. 'The Master Cutler' left for King's Cross via the East Coast Main Line and by the mid-1960s trains to Nottingham were the longest offered. Local services to Aylesbury and London commuter traffic continued to the mid-1980s when closure was threatened. Yet, a reprieve was granted and some ex-Great Western Railway line services were transferred, offering transport to Oxford, Stratford, Kidderminster and Birmingham. Stanier Class 5 no. 44825 has a northbound train for Nottingham during the run-down, February 1966. The engine has lost the shed plate and received the abbreviation 'COLK' for Colwick depot where no. 44825 was employed to the end of the year. A further year was spent at work at Carlisle before withdrawn for scrap. Photograph from the John Day Collection courtesy Rail Photoprints.

Opposite below MARYLEBONE STATION – NO. 9806
At Nationalisation, Robinson A5 Class 4-6-2T no. 9806 has a local train ready to depart Marylebone station. In 1950, the engine transferred to Colwick and was at Gorton before condemned in 1960. Photograph courtesy R.W. Carroll.

Above MOORGATE STATION – NO. 69568

The second stage of the 'North London Railtour' – organised by the Locomotive Club of Great Britain – is soon to depart from Moorgate station to High Barnet via Finsbury Park. Fowler 4P Class 2-6-2T no. 40031 had started the day off from Marylebone, running via Wembley and Willesden to Brentford, then returning north through Twickenham and Richmond to reach Moorgate on the Metropolitan line. The third part of the day took the North London Line through Hackney followed by the Northern & Eastern line to Tottenham via Lea Bridge and terminated at St Pancras with Johnson 3F Class 0-6-0T no. 47202. Photograph courtesy R.W. Carroll.

Opposite MOORGATE STATION – NO. 40022

In the late 1850s, the Metropolitan Railway began a project to connect the northern London termini – Paddington, Euston and King's Cross – with the City. The new decade saw work begin and completed in 1863 with the eastern terminus at Farringdon. Immediately a success, an extension was made to Moorgate, opening in December 1865. In addition, a further set of lines between Farringdon and King's Cross opened during early 1868 and known as the City Widened Lines. At the turn of the century, Moorgate had also connected with the Circle Line and the City & South London Railway which crossed into South London. A mix of steam and electric services are at Moorgate in the 1960s. Later in the decade the station was completely rebuilt as part of the Barbican project. Fowler 3P Class 2-6-2T no. 40022 is about to leave Moorgate with the 17.11 service to St Albans, whilst an underground train from Watford is adjacent on 14th May 1959. Photograph from the Dave Cobbe Collection courtesy Rail Photoprints.

Above NEASDEN SHED – NO. L98

The London Underground celebrated 100 years of services in 1963 and on 25th May an open day was held at Neasden shed. The public is admiring locomotive no. L98 here inside the depot and this had originally opened as a locomotive and carriage works for the Metropolitan Railway in 1882. The engine began life as part of Collett's 5700 Class in January 1930 and was purchased from BR in 1962, continuing work until 1970 when scrapped. Photograph by B.W.L. Brooksbank.

Opposite NEASDEN SHED – NOS L94, L93 AND L48

A trio of London Transport steam engines are at Neasden on 9th September 1961. No. L94 and L93 stand in front of no. L48. Photograph by Hugh Ballantyne courtesy Rail Photoprints.

NINE ELMS SHED

Three Merchant Navy Pacifics are at Nine Elms shed in
1964. Left to right are no. 35030, no. 35023, no. 35013.
Photograph from the Keith Langston Collection
courtesy Rail Photoprints.

NEW CROSS GATE STATION – NO. 32412
The 14.16 freight train to Norwood passes through New Cross Gate station, with assistance in the rear from Billinton E6 Class 0-6-2T no. 32412 on 15th August 1955. Photograph courtesy Rail-Online.

Above NINE ELMS SHED – NO. 31766

The South Eastern main line was provided with new motive power just before the First World War. These were Wainwright L Class 4-4-0s, 12 of which were built by Beyer Peacock & Co. Ltd, whilst an order for ten was placed at Borsig in Germany. Luckily for the South East & Chatham Railway these were completed before the conflict broke out. No. 31766 was the product of the English company in September 1914. The engine looks to have been out of service for some time here at Nine Elms, c. 1960. Arriving at the depot in June 1959 from Faversham, no. 31766 was based there until condemned February 1961. Photograph by Bill Reed.

Opposite above NINE ELMS SHED – NO. 34010

'West Country' Pacific no. 34010 *Sidmouth* emerged into traffic from Brighton Works during September 1945. The engine was 'air smoothed' at this time and later went on to be one of the 60 'light' Pacifics to be rebuilt, with the task being completed in February 1959. In the early 1950s, no. 34010 took employment at Nine Elms and this lasted to late 1964 when a transfer to Eastleigh comprised the engine's last six months in service. Photograph by Bill Reed.

Opposite below NINE ELMS SHED – NO. 32493

In the late 1800s, R.J. Billinton improved his earlier LB&SCR 0-6-2T E3 Class with higher boiler pressure and larger driving wheels to create the E4 Class. The first was introduced in 1897 and production continued to 1903 when 75 had been erected. No. 32493 was new from Brighton Works in November 1899. The engine is pictured at Nine Elms shed during mid-1956 when under two years away from being condemned. Photograph by Bill Reed.

Above NINE ELMS SHED – NO. 34033 AND NO. 34093

Nine Elms was originally the terminus point for the London & Southampton Railway when opened in 1838. Following the extension to Waterloo in the late 1840s, Nine Elms became the location for a large goods depot and railway works. Several engine sheds were also established from the late 1830s to the 1870s. These met their demise before a large half-roundhouse was completed in 1876, followed by a 15-line building in 1885, both south of the main line. The last addition was a 10-track shed in 1910. Exmouth Junction's 'West Country' Pacific no. 34033 *Chard* has been admitted to Nine Elms for attention, as the piston valve is out and the casing is partially removed. Rebuilt 'West Country' Pacific no. 34093 *Saunton* is also in the shed and was based at Nine Elms when captured during 1963. Photograph by Jim Carter courtesy Rail Photoprints.

Opposite NINE ELMS SHED – NO. 34093

With just two days left in traffic, 'West Country' Pacific no. 34093 *Saunton* is at Nine Elms shed for servicing on 7th July 1967. The locomotive was constructed at Brighton Works in October 1949 and rebuilt in May 1960. From 1964 until 1967, no. 34093 was based at Eastleigh. Photograph courtesy Colour-Rail.

NINE ELMS SHED – NO. 30803

'King Arthur' Class 4-6-0 no. 30803 *Sir Harry Le Fise Lake* is on the turntable at Nine Elms on 18th August 1960. Photograph by D.J. Dippie.

Above NINE ELMS SHED – NO. 30768

Coal is sorted in the tender of Urie 'King Arthur' Class 4-6-0 no. 30768 *Sir Balin*. Pictured on 7th September 1960, the engine had worked into the capital from Eastleigh. Photograph by Bill Reed.

Below NINE ELMS SHED – NO. 31768

Another Wainwright L Class 4-4-0 has been pictured at Nine Elms shed. The locomotive is no. 31768 which is seen on 7th September 1960 and was another transfer from Faversham in mid-1959. The locomotive was one of the final class members in service when withdrawn in December 1961. Photograph by Bill Reed.

Above NORTH ACTON – NO. 5014

A train of empty milk wagons is at North Acton behind Collett 'Castle' Class 4-6-0 no. 5014 *Goodrich Castle* on 15th June 1957. The railways had proved revolutionary for the milk industry as rural farmers could quickly dispatch large quantities of produce. Firstly, this was done in milk churns loaded into dedicated vans or those repurposed. In the late 1920s/early 1930s, the traffic was further revolutionised by the introduction of tankers with an approx. 3,000-gallon capacity serving the needs of over 30,000 people. Initially, these had four wheels and no baffles, but an upgrade to six wheels and baffled tanks was soon necessary for stability purposes. The Great Western Railway was the largest mover of dairy and built dedicated vehicles for the movement of churns, whilst the tankers, if built by the 'Big Four', tended to carry private livery. At the height of the traffic, c. 1930, nearly 300 million gallons were transported annually, though by the 1960s this had dramatically declined due to road transport. Photograph by R.C. Riley courtesy Rail-Online.

Below NORWOOD JUNCTION – NO. 32413

Standing at the north end of Norwood Junction station is Billinton E6 Class 0-6-2T no. 32413 on 2nd April 1958. Nearly ten years after the introduction of the E3 Class 0-6-2T for freight duties around London, the modest power of the design was proving troublesome to keep timings along the busy lines. As a result, Billinton repurposed his recent E5 Class designed for passenger duties for the E6 engines. No. 32413 was produced in the middle of the construction programme at Brighton in July 1905. The engine had originally carried no. 413 and named *Fenchurch*, but the latter was removed in August 1911. No. 32413 was allocated to Norwood Junction from October 1953 until condemned during November 1958. Photograph by B.W.L. Brooksbank.

Above NORWOOD JUNCTION SHED – NO. 32337
The first Billinton K Class 2-6-0, no. 32337, stands in the yard at Norwood Junction shed on 6th September 1960. Built at Brighton Works in September 1913, the locomotive was produced in time to assist with the many freight trains running on the LB&SCR's lines following the outbreak of the First World War. Withdrawal occurred at the end of 1962. Marsh C2X no. 32549 is left and classmate no. 32541 is right of no. 32337. Photograph by Bill Reed.

Opposite above OLD OAK COMMON SHED – NO. 4098
Collett 'Castle' Class 4-6-0 no. 4098 *Kidwelly Castle* is at Old Oak Common shed on 16th August 1962. The engine had recently returned to traffic from a period of storage at Newton Abbot and was subsequently allocated to Old Oak Common through to withdrawal in December 1963. Photograph by D.J. Dippie.

Opposite below OLD OAK COMMON SHED – NO. 5931
Old Oak Common depot was a relatively late addition to the Great Western Railway infrastructure. Construction of four roundhouses as part of one complex was completed in 1906, with heavy repair facilities also provided on the site, which was a short distance to the west of Paddington station. The smokebox of Collett 'Hall' Class 4-6-0 no. 5931 *Hatherley Hall* is about to be emptied to the ash pits at the shed on 23rd August 1960. Five years later, Old Oak Common closed to steam but has continued in railway use. Photograph by D.J. Dippie.

Above PADDINGTON STATION – NO. 6169

Following on from the earlier 5101 Class 2-6-2T design from Collett was his own 6100 Class which raised the tractive effort to over 27,000 lb thanks to increased boiler pressure. The 5101 Class originally used 200 lb per sq. in. whilst the 6100s had this set to 225 lb per sq. in. In the first five years of the 1930s, 70 locomotives were completed at Swindon and no. 6169 was amongst these, reaching traffic in November 1935. The class was mainly used around London and no. 6169 is well presented at Paddington station, with first BR emblem, c. 1960. Between 1960 and 1964, no. 6169 was in service at Old Oak Common. Photograph by Bill Reed.

Opposite OLD OAK COMMON – NO. 6132

Empty stock from Paddington reaches Old Oak Common with Collett 6100 Class 2-6-2T no. 6132 on 21st December 1962. In the late 19th century, Old Oak Common was still a relatively rural area, though by the early 1900s the suburbs were quickly swallowing the land. The GWR also took some of this by establishing the engine shed and large carriage sidings on the north side of the main line and just east of the line from Richmond to Willesden Junction. The site continues in railway use at present. Photograph by M. Smith from the Dave Cobbe Collection courtesy Rail Photoprints.

PADDINGTON STATION – NO. 5076

Reversing towards a train at Paddington station on 30th July 1964 is Collett 'Castle' Class no 5076 *Gladiator*. Photograph by Chris Davies courtesy Rail Photoprints.

Above PADDINGTON STATION – NOS 9420 AND 6163
A pair of tank locomotives are engaged at Paddington station during June 1963. On the left is Hawksworth 9400 Class no. 9420 and right is Collett 6100 Class no. 6163. Photograph by David Christie.

Below PADDINGTON STATION – NO. 8433
In October 1963 Hawksworth 9400 Class 0-6-0PT no. 8433 is at Paddington station. Photograph by David Christie.

Above PADDINGTON STATION – NO. 9415
Hawksworth 9400 Class 0-6-0PT no. 9415 has brought a train of empty stock to Paddington on 28th March 1964. Photograph by David Christie.

Below PADDINGTON STATION – NO. 8420
A scene under the train shed at Paddington station featuring Hawksworth 9400 Class no. 8420 which has arrived with a formation of coaches for a subsequent departure on 6th October 1963. Photograph by David Christie.

Above PADDINGTON STATION – NO. 6160
Collett 6100 Class no. 6160 departs for Old Oak Common carriage sidings on 8th August 1964. Two months earlier, the engine had arrived at Southall from Slough. Photograph by David Christie.

Below PADDINGTON STATION – NO. 5058
'Castle' Class 4-6-0 no. 5058 *Earl of Clancarty* reverses away from Paddington after working a train, likely from Gloucester, on 5th September 1962. The first terminus of the GWR was opened to the west of Bishop's Road on 4th June 1838 and this lasted for several years before Brunel's grand station was built. The goods station was established on the site of the original station and this is in the background here. Photograph by David Christie.

Above PADDINGTON STATION – NO. 5055

In 1935, the 100th anniversary for the opening of the line between Paddington and Bristol occurred. To mark this occasion, the GWR introduced the 'Bristolian' between the two places at a schedule of 105 minutes for the 120 miles. The previous fastest train had travelled the route at a mile-a-minute. At the time a seven-carriage formation was in use and initially hauled by a 'King', but later turned over to a 'Castle'. The westbound train left the capital at 10.00, whilst the return was made at 16.30. Removed from the timetable when World War Two started, the 'Bristolian' returned afterwards at a time of 130 minutes. In 1954, the pre-war schedule was reintroduced and on 17th June 1956 'Castle' Class no. 5055 *Earl of Eldon* is ready to take the train out of Paddington. The engine had been named *Lydford Castle* originally. Yet, this was soon lost, as a renaming scheme was instigated following the introduction of the 3200 'Earl' Class 4-4-0s which were thought beneath the standing of their namesakes. No. 5055 was mainly at Old Oak Common from new in June 1936 to 1958 when transferred away. Photograph by Bill Reed.

Above PADDINGTON STATION – NO. 1503

One of the final GWR designs was Hawksworth's 1500 Class 0-6-0PT. Just ten were built at Swindon in 1949 and these were particularly unusual for the type in having outside cylinders. With a short wheelbase also, this left the class with limited functionality and the majority found employment at Old Oak Common shunting stock between there and Paddington. No. 1503 was new in August 1949 and had a role on the aforementioned duty to the end of 1963. The locomotive is arriving at Paddington station here on 17th September 1960. Photograph by Bill Reed.

Above RAYNES PARK STATION – NO. 34098

Pullman cars were introduced to the Bournemouth train by the London & South Western Railway. Though these were later removed, the Southern Railway introduced the 'Bournemouth Belle' train in 1931. Initially a Sunday-only service, by 1936 two services ran daily through to the outbreak of war. Reintroduced in 1946, the formation was ten Pullman carriages, rising to 12 later, with a schedule of just over two hours between Bournemouth West and Waterloo. Stops were made at Bournemouth Central and Southampton Central and the motive power was generally a 'Merchant Navy' Pacific. In this instance, 'West Country' Pacific no. 34098 *Templecombe* has the train at Raynes Park station (south of Wimbledon) in November 1966. Both the train and locomotive did not survive beyond 1967. Photograph courtesy Rail Photoprints.

Opposite PURLEY OAKS – NO. 31872

The 17.25 London Bridge to Reading train passes Purley Oaks on 31st May 1961. The locomotive is Maunsell N Class 2-6-0 no. 31872. Built at Ashford Works in August 1925, the locomotive's service life lasted to May 1963. For the last four years in traffic no. 31872 worked at Redhill depot. Much of the 1950s was spent at work from Bricklayers Arms. Photograph from the Dave Cobbe Collection courtesy Rail Photoprints.

Above RICKMANSWORTH – NO. L95

The Metropolitan line between Rickmansworth and Amersham had to be steam hauled from the 1930s until 1962 as the electrification scheme originally planned was delayed by the Second World War. Work to complete the project is progressing on 4th May 1962 and locomotive no. L95 is engaged near Rickmansworth on an engineer's train. The locomotive was purchased from BR in 1960, being an ex-GWR Collett 5700 Class 0-6-0PT, originally numbered 5764. Photograph by John Briggs courtesy A1 Steam Trust.

Opposite RICKMANSWORTH – NO. 42070

Whilst an exhibition commemorating the demise of steam on London Transport occurred at Neasden, a 'Farewell to Steam' railtour was also organised for 9th September 1961. An electric locomotive began the day at Baker Street station and travelled to Rickmansworth where Fairburn 4P Class 2-6-4T no. 42070 was coupled for the continuation on to Amersham. Over the return the same locomotives were used. The first leg to Amersham is seen departing from Rickmansworth here. Photograph by Hugh Ballantyne courtesy Rail Photoprints.

Above SOUTHALL – NO. 6165
A local train passes through Southall behind Collett 6100 Class 2-6-2T no. 6165 on 13th October 1956. Photograph from the Dave Cobbe Collection courtesy Rail Photoprints.

Opposite above SOUTH KENTON – NO. 48767
Travelling southward along the West Coast Main Line at South Kenton, Stanier 8F no. 48767 has a loaded coal train c. 1960. During the Second World War, Stanier 8F Class 2-8-0s were constructed at works operated by the other three railway companies and then run by them to help ease the burden on their own locomotives. No. 48767 was built at Doncaster Works in March 1946 and worked in LNER territory as Class O6 no. 3162, later no. 3562, until November 1947 when transferred to the LMSR. In the 1950s and early 1960s, the engine mainly worked at Bescot. The Metropolitan Line is seen in the background running over the main line. Photograph from the John Day Collection courtesy Rail Photoprints.

Opposite below SOUTH KENTON – NO. 46433
Ivatt Class 2MT 2-6-0 no. 46433 is Willesden-bound with this freight train, which is passing through South Kenton in July 1950. The locomotive was around 18 months old at this time and had left Crewe Works for Willesden depot. Departing for the North West in 1956, the locomotive's remaining service life was spent in the area at several depots. Photograph by George C. Lander courtesy Rail Photoprints.

Above SOUTHALL – NO. 3799

The GWR made a connection from the main line at Southall to the River Thames at Brentford in the late 1850s. Laid under the guidance of Isambard Kingdom Brunel, the route (and dock facilities) was ready for traffic on 18th July 1859. Primarily a freight route, only two points for passengers to join trains were provided: Brentford; Trumpers Crossing Halte. These both closed during the First World War and again in the second, though permanently. Brentford Dock was closed in 1964 and BR ceased to carry freight on the line in 1970, yet the rails remained for a refuse service which continues to the present. Collett 8750 Class 0-6-0PT no. 3799 comes off the Brentford branch to join the main line with this freight on 16th July 1960. The locomotive was condemned early in 1961. Photograph from the Dave Cobbe Collection courtesy Rail Photoprints.

Below SOUTHALL – NO. 7003

The turntable at Southall shed accommodates Collett 'Castle' Class no. 7011 *Banbury Castle* in 1964. The engine began the year with a move to Worcester and the depot's '85A' code is on the smokebox here, despite the front number plate being missing. The GWR was the only company to retain a separate identity at Grouping in 1923 and the locomotives kept the original number at Nationalisation, whereas the other three had numbers added. No. 7011 moved on to Oxley after six months in Worcester and was condemned there in early 1965. Photograph by A.E. Durrant from the Gordon Edgar Collection courtesy Rail Photoprints.

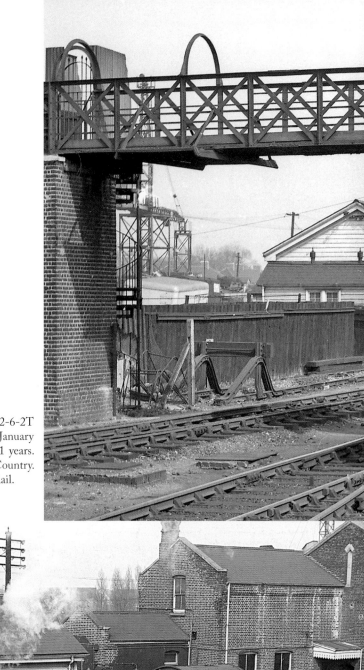

Below SOUTHALL – NO. 6148
At Southall in April 1959 is Collett 6100 Class 2-6-2T no. 6148. Constructed at Swindon Works in January 1933, the locomotive had a service life over 31 years. The last part was spent at work in the West Country. Photograph by F. Hornby courtesy of Colour-Rail.

Above SOUTHALL – NO. 92247

The largest class of BR's Standard designs was the 9F 2-10-0 which was produced to move bulk freight quickly around the country. This simple yet effective aim was undermined by the growing favour of road transport over the railways. Built between 1954 and 1960, the 9Fs numbered 251, yet had particularly short careers due to the acceleration of the dieselisation programme. No. 92247 was amongst the penultimate order of the class constructed at Crewe Works for the Western Region and appeared from there in late 1958. New to Old Oak Common, no. 92247 has a through freight a short distance from there at Southall in April 1959. The locomotive was later at Cardiff and Banbury before transferred to the London Midland Region at Newton Heath where withdrawal occurred in October 1966. Photograph courtesy Colour-Rail.

ST PANCRAS STATION – NO. 45274
In May 1958, Stanier Class 5 no. 45274 has an express at St Pancras station with Jubilee no. 45618 *New Hebrides* to the right. Photograph courtesy Colour-Rail.

Above ST PANCRAS STATION – NO. 160 AND NO. M161

On 10th June 1948, two Stanier 3Ps – no. 160 and no. M161 – are ready to move used stock out of St Pancras station. Photograph by B.W.L. Brooksbank.

Below ST PANCRAS STATION – NO. 45614

On 18th March 1961, Stanier 'Jubilee' Class no. 45614 *Leeward Islands* has an early morning express at St Pancras station. Allocated to Kentish Town at the time, a move to Derby took place at the end of the year. Photograph by B.W.L. Brooksbank.

Above ST PANCRAS STATION – NO. 73142

The 10.50 express to Leicester is at the platform and ready for departure from St Pancras station on 13th June 1957. BR Standard Class 5 4-6-0 no. 73142, which was one of thirty fitted with British Caprotti valve gear, is the six-month-old engine in charge of the train. Photograph by B.W.L. Brooksbank.

Opposite above ST PANCRAS STATION – NO. 45605

After Grouping, the LMSR failed to keep pace with the express engines on competitor lines, such as the Gresley A1 Pacific and the Collett 'Castle' Classes. The LMSR relied on inadequate 4-4-0s and uneconomical 4-6-0s. Fowler's 'Royal Scot' Class was a step in the right direction, yet further action was needed. W.A. Stanier was specially recruited from the GWR to significantly upgrade the LMSR stock in 1931. Initially finding his feet in the role, the first significant design was the 'Princess Royal' Pacific of 1933. He later turned to a 4-6-0 for secondary expresses and the first 'Jubilee' appeared in 1934. For both designs he hampered himself by favouring a small superheater, as was the case on the GWR, when others had proved a suitably large superheater was necessary. Consequently, modifications were necessary to boiler specifications before the right arrangement was found. Many were built with a domeless boiler with straight firebox throatplate and 14-element superheater. The standard adopted subsequently was a domed boiler with sloping firebox throatplate, slightly increasing the grate area, and 21-element superheater. No. 45605 *Cyprus* was amongst the last built with the original specification at the North British Locomotive Company in April 1935. The engine is at St Pancras station on 22nd August 1957 with a Leeds-bound express. Photograph by K.C.H. Fairey courtesy of Colour-Rail.

Opposite below ST PANCRAS STATION – NO. 70052

A Locomotive Club of Great Britain railtour is ready to leave St Pancras station on 24th April 1965. BR Standard Class 7 'Britannia' Pacific no. 70052 *Firth of Tay* was to deliver the party to Nottingham and hand over to an Ivatt Class 4, as well as Thompson B1 for the tour's main event of a journey around Nottinghamshire and Lincolnshire. No. 70052 remained on hand at Nottingham to return the club members back to St Pancras. Photograph by L. Rowe courtesy of Colour-Rail.

Above ST PANCRAS STATION – NO. 44667

Stanier Class 5 no. 44667 arrives at St Pancras station with the 'Derby Holiday Express', c. 1960. The locomotive was built at Crewe Works in July 1949 and lasted to August 1967. In the early 1960s, the engine was employed in the Midlands at Leicester, then moving to the ex-GC at Woodford Halse and Leicester. Returning to the London Midland Region in late 1963, no. 44667 had spells at Lancaster and Carnforth before condemned. Photograph by D. Preston courtesy of Colour-Rail.

Opposite ST PANCRAS STATION – NO. 45514

Fifty-two Fowler 'Patriot' Class 4-6-0s were constructed to assist the 'Royal Scot' Class on the LMSR expresses. Like the latter engines, the 'Patriots' were rebuilt with Stanier features, though in a smaller quantity. Eighteen transformations took place between 1946 and 1949. No. 45514 *Holyhead* was constructed at Crewe Works in September 1932 and later rebuilt in March 1947. The engine was the first of the group to be withdrawn in May 1961 and is pictured under a year earlier at St Pancras station on 20th August 1960. Photograph by D.J. Dippie.

Above STEPNEY EAST STATION – NO. 42501

The last steam-hauled train between Fenchurch Street and Southend passes through Stepney East station on 15th June 1962. Opened by the Commercial Railway (later London & Blackwall Railway) in 1840, Stepney East was later the place of a junction for a connection to the GER at Bow. This was used by the London, Tilbury & Southend Railway to reach Fenchurch Street station, avoiding the busy lines through Stratford. After the Second World War, Stepney East was electrified as part of the LNER's suburban electrification scheme and the LT&SR project was completed for mid-1962. This train is headed by Stanier 4P no. 42501, which was a long-term servant of the line. Photograph by K.L. Cook from Rail Archive Stephenson courtesy Rail-Online.

Opposite STEWARTS LANE – NO. 30901

Just south of Victoria station at Stewarts Lane, near the locomotive shed, 'Schools' Class no. 30901 *Winchester* is on standby for a royal train working on 8th June 1962. Following Nationalisation, the 'School' Class continued to wear Malachite green livery of the Southern Railway, then when BR chose the standard liveries, lined black was applied. No. 30901 was an early repaint in late 1948, also receiving the 'British Railways' lettering on the tender. From June 1956, the class began to have Brunswick green livery and this has been brought to a high standard here for the working. The BR standard for nameplates was a black background, yet this was not enforced rigorously as many engine sheds favoured a red background which is the case here. No. 30901 survived to the end of the year. Photograph from the Dave Cobbe Collection courtesy Rail Photoprints.

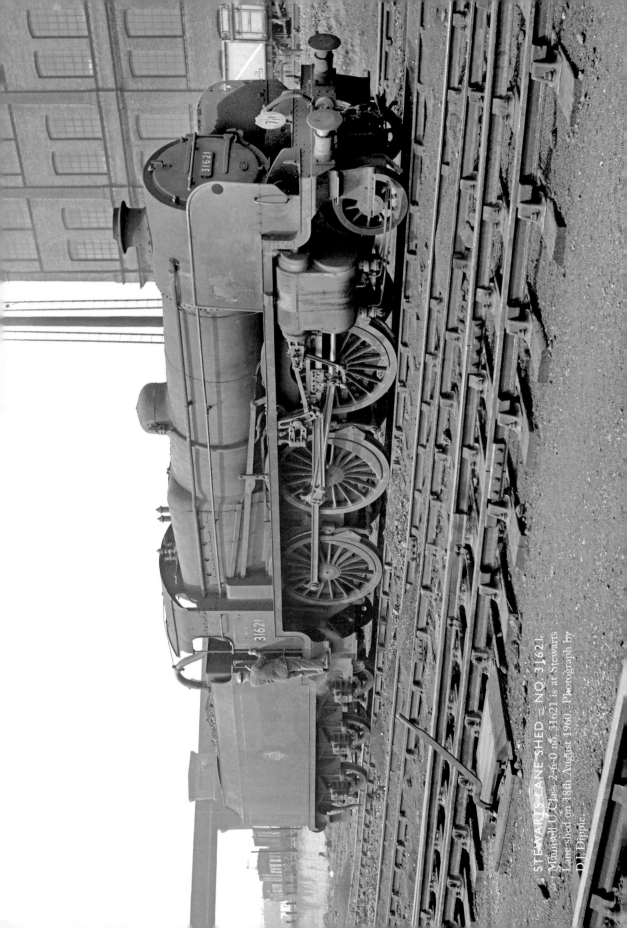

STEWARTS LANE SHED — NO. 31621.

Maunsell U Class 2-6-0 no. 31621 is at Stewarts Lane shed on 18th August 1960. Photograph by D.J. Dippie.

Above STEWARTS LANE SHED – NO. 75070
Three Bridges-allocated BR Standard Class 4 4-6-0 no. 75070 stands in the yard at Stewarts Lane shed, with 'Schools' Class no. 30923 *Bradfield* left. Photograph by D.J. Dippie.

Below STEWARTS LANE SHED – NO. 34083
Bulleid 'Battle of Britain' Pacific no. 34083 *605 Squadron* is 'on shed' at Stewarts Lane before working back home to Dover on 18th August 1960. Photograph by D.J. Dippie.

Above STEWARTS LANE SHED – NO. 30921

The London, Chatham & Dover Railway established stabling facilities for locomotives at Battersea in 1862. Also known as Longhedge and Battersea, Stewarts Lane shed was originally a half-roundhouse before a large new depot was erected in the 1880s. This continued to serve steam to 1963 when given over to diesel maintenance. 'Schools' Class no. 30921 *Shrewsbury* is outside the shed building on 6th September 1960. Photograph by Bill Reed.

Opposite STRATFORD

The Eastern Counties Railway established a railway workshop at Romford in the early 1840s. The company required more space and relocated into London, taking an old engine shed at Stratford which was between the Cambridge line and that to Colchester, Ipswich and Norwich. Operations soon expanded and locomotives were built and repaired there, as well as carriages and wagons. The last-mentioned vehicles were later built a short distance away at Temple Mills where dedicated facilities were created. Over 1,700 engines were erected and more than 5,000 carriages during the heyday of the workshops. At the end of steam, diesel locomotives were repaired until the site closed in 1991. A line of inactive engines is at Stratford on 17th August 1962. Worsdell J15 Class 0-6-0 no. 65469 is nearest. Photograph by D.J. Dippie.

Above STRATFORD SHED – NO. 64657
Hill J19 Class 0-6-0 no. 64657 stands on the ash pits at Stratford shed c. 1960. The locomotive was at the depot for the last 18 months in service. Photograph by Bill Reed.

Below STRATFORD SHED – NO. 69709
Apparently out of service (note the chain winch attached to the handrail) at Stratford shed c. 1960 is Hill N7 Class 0-6-2T no. 69709. Photograph by Bill Reed.

Above STRATFORD WORKS – NO. 61668

A day after officially condemned, Gresley B17 Class 4-6-0 no. 61668 *Bradford City* stands outside Stratford Works on 23rd August 1960. The locomotive was amongst the final batch of B17s erected by Robert Stephenson & Co., entering traffic in April 1937. The North Eastern Area of the LNER was initially to accept some of the later engines, though this was dropped and the B17s went to the Great Central Section. As a result, a Group Standard 4,200-gallon tender was provided, as well as vacuum brakes fitted. Yet, no. 61668 soon transferred to the Great Eastern Section and had Westinghouse brake equipment provided (seen here left). Photograph by D.J. Dippie.

Above SURBITON STATION – NO. 73114

On the London & Southampton Railway line when opened in 1838, Surbiton station was originally named Kingston for Kingston-upon-Thames which originally rejected the chance to be served by the company. The presence of the railway prompted the development of Surbiton as a suburban settlement. The station formally became Surbiton in October 1867 and was completely rebuilt during the 1930s in the Art Deco style to the design of Southern Railway architect James Robb Scott. BR Standard Class 5 no. 73114 *Etarre* is at Surbiton with the 11.30 Waterloo to Bournemouth West on 18th February 1962. Also in the station is N Class 2-6-0 no. 31811 which is working on an engineer's train – the fresh ballast is visible. Photograph by Ian Turnbull courtesy Rail Photoprints.

Below
SURBITON STATION – NO. 34052
Bulleid 'Battle of Britain' Pacific no. 34052 *Lord Dowding* is on the through line at Surbiton station c. 1960. The engine was reconstructed at Eastleigh Works in September 1958 and was amongst the final steam withdrawals in July 1967. No. 34052 was employed at Salisbury from 1951. Photograph courtesy R.W. Carroll.

VAUXHALL – NO. 35014
Merchant Navy Pacific no. 35014 *Nederland Line* has the southbound Atlantic Coast Express at Vauxhall on 31st May 1962. Photograph from the Dave Cobbe Collection courtesy Rail Photoprints.

Above UPMINSTER – NO. 42527

The 11.48 Fenchurch Street to Southend departs from Upminster on 21st July 1957. The locomotive is Stanier three-cylinder 4P no. 42527. Photograph by K.L. Cook from Rail Archive Stephenson courtesy Rail-Online.

Below SURBITON – NO. 34095

A Waterloo to Bournemouth West express hauled by rebuilt 'West Country' Pacific no. 34095 *Brentor* is viewed from King Charles Road bridge on 4th June 1965. Photograph by B.W.L. Brooksbank.

Above VICTORIA STATION – NO. 80085
BR Standard Class 4 2-6-4T no. 80085 stands at Victoria station's platform 14 with the 12.03 to Brighton via Oxted and East Grinstead on 7th June 1954. To the left are the carriages forming the 'Brighton Belle' Pullman train. Photograph by B.W.L. Brooksbank.

Below VICTORIA STATION – NO. 70004
On 5th September 1953 'Britannia' Pacific no. 70004 *William Shakespeare* has the 'Golden Arrow' boat train at Victoria station. Photograph by B.W.L. Brooksbank.

Above VAUXHALL – NO. 443

A train of empty milk wagons approaches Vauxhall station after depositing the contents at the nearby United Dairies facility. Drummond T14 Class 4-6-0 no. 443 still carries the identity of the Southern Railway on 24th April 1948. Photograph by B.W.L. Brooksbank.

Below VAUXHALL STATION – NO. 30321

A train of empty stock has been collected at Clapham Junction and bound for Waterloo. The set is at Vauxhall station behind Drummond M7 Class 0-4-4T no. 30321 on 6th April 1962. Photograph by B.W.L. Brooksbank.

Above WATERLOO STATION – NO. 30453

Robert Urie retired when the London & South Western Railway became a constituent of the Southern Railway at Grouping and Richard Maunsell moved up from the South East & Chatham Railway to be Chief Mechanical Engineer. He went on to design the 'Lord Nelson' 4-6-0s, yet an immediate need for locomotives resulted in the construction of more Urie N15 Class 'King Arthurs'. Some of these featured reclaimed parts from Drummond's failed four-cylinder 4-6-0s, including no. 30453 *King Arthur*. The locomotive was one of ten built at Eastleigh Works in 1925 and was completed there in February. At the head of the 14.54 stopping train to Basingstoke on 11th May 1959, no. 30453 was a long-term resident of Salisbury shed and had the depot's '72B' on the smokebox door. Withdrawal from there occurred in July 1961. Photograph by B.W.L. Brooksbank.

Opposite above WATERLOO STATION – NO. 414

Between 1903 and 1907, 40 Drummond L11 Class 4-4-0s were built by the L&SWR for passenger and freight work. No. 414 was the last of five built at Nine Elms Works in July 1906. The engine is pictured at Waterloo station on 24th June 1950 and was under a year away from being condemned at Yeovil Town. The class was withdrawn between 1949 and 1952. Photograph by B.W.L. Brooksbank.

Opposite below WATERLOO – NO. 34027

A connection between the London & South Western Railway and South Eastern Railway was deemed desirable by the latter company in the early 1860s. Following the opening of the extension from London Bridge to Charing Cross, a station was built on the eastern side of Waterloo and began serving passengers from January 1869 as Waterloo Junction. A single line connected the two stations and was in use until 1916. Bulleid 'West Country' Pacific no. 34027 *Taw Valley* is on the line from Charing Cross to Waterloo Junction (known as just Waterloo from 1935 and later Waterloo East in 1977) here on 11th May 1959 with the 15.08 train to Deal. Construction of the 'Downstream' building of the Shell Centre is proceeding on the right. No. 34027 was later preserved and is currently operational on the Severn Valley Railway, though not mainline certified. Photograph by B.W.L. Brooksbank.

Above WATERLOO STATION – NO. 73022

Two-and-a-quarter miles of track were controlled by Waterloo signal box, which sits behind BR Standard Class 5 no. 73022. Constructed in 1936, the box had 309 levers and electrically operated track circuits, with a large display showing the various movements in the vicinity. Over 1,000 movements occurred daily and at peak times seven trains left Waterloo every five minutes. The box stood until the early 1990s when work began on adapting the station for the Channel Tunnel traffic. No. 73022 is at Waterloo on 3rd July 1966 after a recent move from Guildford to Nine Elms shed. Constructed at Derby Works in October 1951, the engine originally went to the London Midland Region before taken on by the Western Region from 1953 to 1965. Photograph by David Christie.

Opposite WATERLOO STATION – NO. 82028

At Nationalisation, several areas had a requirement for a medium-distance locomotive which was powerful but had a relatively low axle load. The LMSR had no suitable modern vehicle, resulting in BR turning to the GWR 2-6-2T classes for inspiration. The Standard Class 3 2-6-2T was built at Swindon Works between 1952 and 1955, numbering 45 examples. No. 82028 was built there in December 1954 and delivered to Darlington shed for work in the North Eastern Region. The engine also had spells at Scarborough, Malton and York before transferred to the Southern Region in September 1963. In October 1961, no. 82028 came to grief whilst working a ballast train approaching Robin Hood's Bay. The train ran away and was diverted into a siding, with the locomotive crashing into the buffers. The location proved difficult to salvage the engine and two weeks elapsed before the retrieval was complete. No. 82028 is at Waterloo station looking similarly the worse for wear on 3rd March 1966. The locomotive survived several months longer to September. Photograph courtesy Rail-Online.

Above WATERLOO STATION – NO. 35005

The 'Bournemouth Belle' is at Waterloo during July 1964 with 'Merchant Navy' Class Pacific no. 35005 *Canadian Pacific*. Constructed at Eastleigh Works in December 1941, the engine was in original 'air smoothed' form until May 1959 when reconstructed to BR specifications. In the 1950s, the engine's time was split between Exmouth Junction and Nine Elms, reaching Bournemouth at the end of 1959. No. 35005 had a year at Weymouth until condemned during October 1965, later being preserved after rescue from Barry Scrapyard. Returning to steam in the 1990s, *Canadian Pacific* ran for around 20 years on the mainline and at private lines. A second restoration is currently taking place. Photograph courtesy R.W. Carroll.

Opposite above WATERLOO STATION – NO. 34046

'West Country' Pacific no. 34046 *Braunton* is at the head of an express ready to leave Waterloo station on 9th June 1963. The engine was Bournemouth-allocated at the time and was condemned there in October 1965. Rebuilding took place in February 1959 just before the move from Brighton to Bournemouth occurred. Photograph by David Christie.

Opposite below WATERLOO STATION – NO. 34018

Eastleigh's 'West Country' Pacific no. 34018 *Axminster* stands with a train at Waterloo station on 5th May 1966. In the following month, the locomotive was posted to the capital at Nine Elms which remained the case until sent for scrap in July 1967. Photograph by Bill Wright.

Above WATERLOO STATION – NO. 80015

Originally intended to be a temporary terminus before an extension further east was made, Waterloo station opened to traffic as Waterloo Bridge on 11th July 1848. As this proved the end point for the L&SWR, several additions were made on site before a rebuilding project was undertaken in the early 20th century. Interrupted by the First World War, the works ended just before Grouping at a cost of around £2 million. The station was later modernised for Eurostar services, though in 2007 these were transferred to St Pancras. BR Standard Class 4 2-6-4T no. 80015 is light engine at Waterloo on 5th May 1966. Photograph by Bill Wright.

Opposite above WATERLOO STATION – NO. 30520

The main tower of the Shell Centre dominates this view of Waterloo station, taken c. 1960. When completed in 1962, the building stood 351 ft tall with 27 stories and was for a time the tallest building in Britain before that accolade was claimed by the CIS Tower in Manchester. In the foreground is another Urie H15 engaged on empty stock movements, no. 30520 of Feltham. Photograph by Bill Reed.

Opposite below WATERLOO STATION – NO. 30585 AND NO. 30587

The L&SWR introduced 2-4-0WT locomotives for London suburban traffic in the mid-19th century and when later superseded these were distributed away to other points of the system. In the 1890s, a trio found employment on the Bodmin & Wadebridge Railway for china clay trains which had to negotiate severe track restrictions. No other designs could be used, meaning these engines survived several decades longer than their class mates. Two Beattie 0298 Class 2-4-0WT locomotives have returned to the capital for a special train at the end of their nearly 90-year career on 2nd December 1962. A joint railtour was organised by the Stephenson Locomotive Society and Railway Correspondence & Travel Society to run behind the pair from Waterloo to Hampton Court and return via Richmond. Both locomotives were subsequently preserved. Photograph by Bill Reed.

WEMBLEY – NO. 70047
Early in 1963, with sanders working, 'Britannia' Pacific no. 70047 (never named) has a northbound relief express at Wembley. Photograph courtesy Rail Photoprints.

Above WATERLOO STATION – NO. 34063
Original 'Battle of Britain' Pacific no. 34063 *229 Squadron* is at Waterloo with an express c. 1955. For much of the 1950s, the engine worked from Nine Elms depot. Photograph by Peter Gale.

Below WATERLOO STATION – NO. 35022
One of the early 'Merchant Navy' rebuilds was no. 35022 *Holland America Line* in late 1956. The locomotive is at Waterloo during the late 1950s. Photograph by Peter Gale.

WEST EALING – NO. 4706
A permanent way train, with pre-made rail and sleeper sections, is at West Ealing with Churchward 4700 Class 2-8-0 no. 4706 on 28th November 1959. Photograph by K.L. Cook from Rail Archive Stephenson courtesy Rail-Online.

Above WEMBLEY – NO. 67774
Visitors to Wembley stadium could be deposited at one of three stations near the site. Wembley Stadium station was on a loop between the GC main line and the branch from Neasden to Northolt Junction. Thompson L1 no. 67774 has a train on the loop here. Photograph courtesy R.W. Carroll.

Below WEST GREEN STATION – NO. 69625
On the Palace Gates branch at West Green station, Hill N7 Class no. 69625 has a local service, c. 1955. The short line closed in 1964. Photograph courtesy R.W. Carroll.

Above WILLESDEN SHED

Willesden was an important point as several lines connected with each other: West Coast Main Line; North London line; West London line; North & South Western Junction Railway. As a result, large sidings, carriage sheds and locomotive depot existed there. Willesden shed was built by the LNWR in 1873 and was a 12-road straight building. This was extended at the turn of the century, then a roundhouse was constructed by the LMSR in 1929. The extension was later demolished leaving the original structure standing and this is pictured here in October 1964. In the foreground is Fowler 3F 0-6-0T no. 47501, which was soon to be withdrawn, behind to the left stands Ivatt 4MT 2-6-0 no. 43019 ready to return to Stoke and left is BR Standard Class 5 no. 73014. The latter was amongst a relatively small number of that class to wear BR Brunswick green livery as the standard was black with lining. No. 73014 was painted at Eastleigh earlier in 1964 and the works differed from others in applying the orange lining bands to the running plate all along the top and bottom edges. Willesden shed was open to late August 1965. Photograph courtesy Rail Photoprints.

Opposite WILLESDEN SHED

The yard at Willesden shed is busy on 10th June 1964. On the left is BR Standard Class 2 2-6-0 no. 78039 which was based at the depot from May 1963 to October 1965. The engine was new to Rhyl in November 1954 and had 18 months there before a transfer to Widnes occurred. To the right stands BR Standard Class 5 no. 73033. Three months earlier, the locomotive worked at Willesden but moved on to Bletchley until the end of the year. An LMSR tank, Stanier 8F and Class 5 are also present, as well as a 'Britannia' Pacific in the top left corner. Photograph by Hugh Ballantyne courtesy Rail Photoprints.

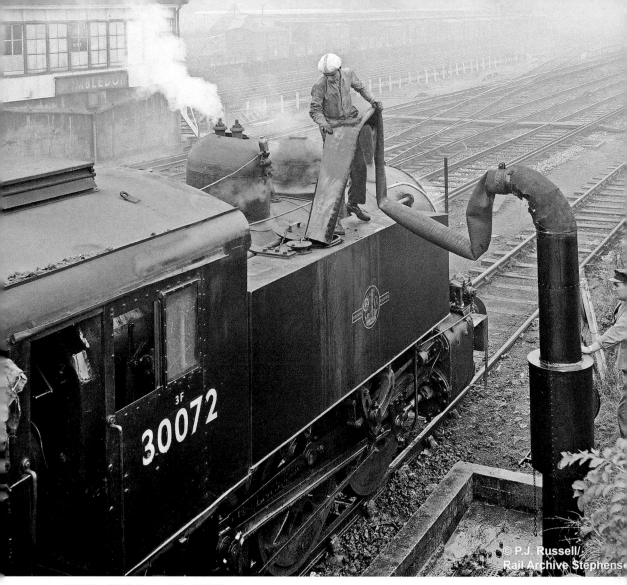

Above WIMBLEDON – NO. 30072

The Southern Railway purchased surplus US Army S100 0-6-0T locomotives for work at Southampton Docks following the Second World War. Fulfilling this duty ably until dieselisation in 1962, a new role had to be found for a number of class members. No. 30072 was sent to Guildford and became the shed pilot until the end of steam and was later preserved. The locomotive is seen here taking water at Wimbledon before working the Southern Counties Touring Society's 'Four Counties' railtour on 9th October 1966. As the class had a tendency to run hot on long journeys, no. 30072 was only used on a short portion along the Merton Abbey branch from Wimbledon to Tooting Junction. Photograph by P.J. Russell from Rail Archive Stephenson courtesy Rail-Online.

Opposite above WIMBLEDON STATION – NO. 34013

A northbound express has reached Wimbledon station on 6th July 1967. This was one of 'West Country' Pacific no. 34013 *Okehampton*'s final duties as withdrawal soon occurred. Photograph courtesy R.W. Carroll.

Opposite below WIMBLEDON – NO. 35016

Bulleid 'Merchant Navy' Pacific no. 35016 *Elders Fyffes* approaches Wimbledon with an express in 1954. Reconstruction took place at Eastleigh in April 1957 and the locomotive continued in traffic to August 1965. On the left is Durnsford Road EMU shed. Photograph from the John Day Collection courtesy Rail Photoprints.

BIBLIOGRAPHY

Allen, C.J. *Titled Trains of Great Britain*. 1983.

Bradley, D.L. *Locomotives of the Southern Railway Part One*. 1975.

Bradley, D.L. *Locomotives of the Southern Railway Part Two*. 1976.

Bradley, D.L. *Locomotives of the L.S.W.R. Part One*. 1965.

Bradley, D.L. *Locomotives of the L.S.W.R. Part Two*. 1967.

Bradley, D.L. *Locomotives of the L.B.&S.C.R. Part Three*. 1974.

Bradley, D.L. *The Locomotives of the South Eastern & Chatham Railway*. 1965.

Dow, George. *Great Central Volumes 1-3*. 1985.

Ellaway, K.J. *The Great British Railway Station: Euston*. 1994.

Griffiths, Roger and Paul Smith. *The Directory of British Engine Sheds and Principal Locomotive Servicing Points: 1 Southern England, the Midlands, East Anglia and Wales*. 1999.

Hawkins, Chris and George Reeve. *An Historical Survey of Southern Sheds*. 2001.

Quick, Michael. *Railway Passenger Stations in Great Britain: A Chronology*. 2009.

RCTS. *A Detailed History of British Railways Standard Steam Locomotives Volumes 1-4*. 2007-2008.

RCTS. *Locomotives of the LNER. Parts 1-10A*.

Sixsmith, Ian. *The Book of the Royal Scots*. 2008.

Swift, Peter. *Locomotives in Detail Six: Maunsell 4-4-0 Schools Class*. 2006.

Thorne, Robert. *Liverpool Street Station*. 1978.

Townsin, Ray. *The Jubilee 4-6-0s*. 2006.

Walmsley, Tony. *Shed by Shed Part One: London Midland*. 2010.

Walmsley, Tony. *Shed by Shed Part Two: Eastern*. 2010.

Walmsley, Tony. *Shed by Shed Part Five: Southern*. 2008.

White, H.P. *A Regional History of the Railways of Great Britain, Volume 3 – Greater London*. 1963.

Wrottesley, John. *The Great Northern Railway: Volumes 1-3*. 1979-1981.

Also available from Great Northern

The Last Years of Yorkshire Steam

The Golden Age of Yorkshire Railways

Gresley's A3s

Peppercorn's Pacifics

London Midland Steam 1948-1966

The Last Years of North East Steam

British Railways Standard Pacifics

Western Steam 1948-1966

The Last Years of North West Steam

Gresley's V2s

Southern Steam 1948-1967

Yorkshire Steam 1948-1967

Gresley's A4s

Gresley's B17s

The Last Years of West Midlands Steam

East Midlands Steam 1950-1966

Thompson's B1s

The Glorious Years of the LNER

Scottish Steam 1948-1967

North East Steam 1948-1968

Gresley's D49s

visit www.*greatnorthernbooks.co.uk* for details.